Rise Up!

Rise Up!

Uncover the Darkness, Move into the Light,
and Experience a Life of Joy!

Part of the #iJOY Series

Brenda Epperson-Moore

Foreword by Bodie Thoene

RESOURCE *Publications* · Eugene, Oregon

RISE UP!
Uncover the Darkness, Move into the Light, and Experience a Life of Joy!

Resource Publications
An Imprint of Wipf and Stock Publishers
199 W. 8th Ave., Suite 3
Eugene, OR 97401

www.wipfandstock.com

PAPERBACK ISBN: 978-1-7252-9424-0
HARDCOVER ISBN: 978-1-7252-9425-7
EBOOK ISBN: 978-1-7252-9426-4

03/16/21

Contents

Foreword by Bodie Thoene | vii

Preface | ix

Book Overview | xiii

Acknowledgements | xv

Joy | 1

1. *Joy* In Pain | 3

2. Childhood Interrupted | 13

3. Breaking into Mercy | 24

4. Be Bold, Don't Lose Hope | 35

5. When Did Life Become So Serious? | 45

6. Don't Confuse Small with Insignificant | 53

7. Keep Dreaming | 59

8. Hurry Up So You Can Slow Down | 66

9. Ready Or Not Here I Come | 76

10. When the Impossible Becomes Possible | 85

11. I was Young and Very Restless | 92

Perseverance | 101

12. Removing Toxic Thoughts and People | 103

13. Generational Hope | 111

14. Finding Love in the Prayer Closet | 118

15. My "Book of Promises" | 128

16. Pulling the Weeds | 138

17. Help, There's a Teenager in My House | 143

18. Staying Plugged In | 150

19. Racing against Time | 158

Trust | 169

20. The Great Awakening | 171

Author's Platform | 181

About the Author | 183

Bibliography | 185

Foreword

RISE UP!, THE STORY of Brenda Epperson-Moore's life, unpacks the challenge of finding great joy no matter what the circumstances.

My dear friend Brenda is known and loved around the world for her portrayal of Ashley Abbott on CBS's daytime drama, *The Young and the Restless*. Millions admire her, but only now, by sharing her memories, will they truly understand her strength, her courage, and her boundless faith. Beyond her 'reel' life, there is so much more to her "real" life.

The truth of Brenda's story is a drama about overcoming tragedy and rising up through deep faith in God.

Personally, whenever I'm in need, Brenda is the first person I call and ask for prayer and counsel. In reading *Rise Up!*, I knew the pages of this incredible book would bring that same deep sense of trustworthy friendship straight to the heart of the reader.

It's the next best thing to calling Brenda at midnight and saying, "Pray for me!"

Rise Up! is a story of finding joy even in the midst of physical danger. When the recent wild fires swept through California, Brenda was on the front lines, helping first responders, friends, neighbors, and strangers escape. With the flames at her back, she fearlessly loaded her stock trailer and transported animals out of the danger zone as she prayed for physical protection. Her beautiful songs of praise could be heard as she drove through the smoke and desolation.

Rise Up! is also the story of conquering the spiritual wild fires in life. From a childhood touched by tragedy, Brenda rose from the ashes to become a world changer. She radiates the joy of one who has walked through tribulation and emerged on the other side with the testimony that Jesus Christ has walked with her every step of the way.

Foreword

    Rise Up! is a book for everyone who longs to live a life of contentment and peace. Brenda's beautiful story is proof for everyone who reads it that nothing is impossible with God!

    Rise Up! is a life changer; the story of the decade!

    Read *Rise Up!* and you'll never be the same. Then buy copies for everyone you know and love. Pass it on! It will rock your world and theirs.

Bodie Thoene

Preface

ONE LIFE CAN MAKE *a difference through God's power and grace. "Rise Up!"* *chronicles Brenda Epperson-Moore's inspirational journey through childhood* *tragedy to* joy *and freedom. When tragic circumstances catapulted Brenda* *into some of her darkest hours, God's love and grace revealed how to trans-* *form her pain into victory and* joy. *As she discovered the miraculous power* *of prayer, the word of God, and absolute faith in God and His promises, the* *darkness turned to light, and her new-found path of hope took her to un-* *imaginable heights, in which she discovered God's limitless possibilities.*

I tried everything possible to avoid writing this book; I really did. I tried simply not doing it, I tried running from God, but ultimately, His will be done.

Several years ago I started feeling this inner calling to write my story, to share with people how God took me from being a size 16, out of control and angry youth, a victim of sexual assault, rage, and the onset of diabetes, who grew up with a single mom who sometimes did not know where our next meal was coming from, to the *joy*ous person who I am today: married to the love of my life, raising three beautiful daughters, enjoying a success-ful career as a singer, actress, and speaker.

Writing a book was the last thing I wanted to do when I felt God nudging me. I wondered what I could possibly say that would somehow help anyone? I knew writing a book would take all of me and more, and I just wasn't having it.

Have you ever tried to ignore God?

Out of the blue, friends would call me and say, "Brenda, I feel so strongly that you need to write a book." A few years ago, a stranger I had never met told me when we were praying together at a disaster site where people had been killed by an active shooter, "You have wisdom, a voice, and people need to hear what you have to say, so speak." I was stunned. Little did he know this was something I was battling with over the years. I took what the stranger said into my heart and silently said a prayer of agreement over his words.

I knew it was time.

So that's my "why."

Rise Up! is a book about *joy*, a deep inner *joy* I could have never achieved without God's grace and mercy. By the time you've reached the end of this book, I believe you're going to identify what's holding you back and move forward to reach solutions in your life like I had to do. You will build your faith, break chains, and the negative ideas you have about yourself will no longer have a stronghold over your life. Those thoughts and lies will be replaced with the powerful truth of who you are and *joy* will begin to *Rise Up* on the inside of you. You will receive practical tools and biblical principles that will ignite a new flame of hope in your life.

Tragedy in my childhood years catapulted me into some of my darkest hours. My father, famed musician and actor Don Epperson, suffered an untimely death when I was six years old. I was also the victim of sexual assault by a family friend as a child at age six; my secret held a powerful grip over me as I seethed with unforgiveness and anger. After the rape, I became a diabetic. I had a horrible relationship with food, and I was excessively overweight; by fifth grade, I was a size 16 and 180 pounds. My mother was a single mom who sometimes picked fruit in the fields to provide for us. Forces of rage, darkness, and hate slept in my bed and haunted my thoughts every night. As a nine-year-old in deep pain, I raised my fist at the sky and said, "I hate you, God."

When I spoke those horrible words I felt a "shift." I believe at that moment a stronghold of bitterness and anger came into my life and heart. My unchecked anger left me lonely, friendless, an outcast, fat, and the school principal's worst nightmare.

After I accepted Christ into my heart at nine years old, I began to crave the word of God.

I had an insatiable desire to read my Bible almost every day, I wanted to go to church, and I began to envision myself in faraway lands helping people I did not know and had never seen. I figured if God can do anything and He is the inside of me, then so can I. I would finally begin to see myself as God saw me—*limitless*.

Today my life is a testament to my faith. I received worldwide recognition through the eight years I played Ashley Abbott on CBS's daytime drama, *The Young and the Restless*. I was signed as a musical artist with

Sony/TriStar Music label and I became the opening act for Lionel Richie's world tour. That is not to say that I did not have to do the work to find my *joy*. I'm also a breast cancer survivor. I've overcome financial ruin, rape, and a devastating divorce, as well as three calamitous miscarriages.

I want you to know that no matter how lost, angry, or confused you are, you can forgive, move forward, and still find *joy*. It's going to take some inner work, but it's a beautiful journey, a path I wouldn't have changed for anything. God will use the smallest of prayers in a mighty way.

Joy is a state of mind and an orientation of the heart. It is a settled state of contentment, confidence, and hope. *Joy* is different from happiness. Happiness is a temporary emotion, while *joy* is a state of mind, a decision

My book will teach you how to use what God has given you and what life sometimes hands you, then make a decision to *RISE UP* in *joy* anyway, even in the midst of a blowing storm.

I'm going to show you how God's mercy can bring you:

Joy in your relationship with God

Joy in yourself

Joy in your everyday life

Joy in your family

Joy in your work

Joy in life

My whole life people have been telling me, "Shhh. You talk too loud. You're too much of a tomboy, too much of a rebel."

When the fires and pandemic hit, God gave me such an unshakable confidence in myself and in Him that no one was going to tell me to be quiet anymore. I'm a rockstar in the kingdom of God, and no one or nothing is going to dim my shine. God says, "If I have done something for you, shout it from the rooftops. 'What you have said in the dark, will be heard in the light'" (Luke 12:3 ESV).

My goal with this book is to encourage everyone who has ever experienced loss, rejection, anger, loneliness, anxiety, hopelessness, doubt, physical limitation, insecurity, or injustice to realize that *nothing is impossible with God*. The promise of God's healing power is real.

Live like salt and light in a dark world. I believe this book will build up your faith muscle. Never stop praying, being kind, doing what's right; never stop believing that your life can have an impact, and be full and filled with glory and *joy* unspeakable. IJOY, we're all in this together!

By the time you finish this book, you'll be doing a "*joy* wave."

Book Overview

THIS BOOK IS FOR readers in the category similar to *I Dare to Call Him Father, I Dreamed Freedom,* the *Pursuit of Happyness,* and *God's Promise of Happiness.* A remarkable story about a sensitive young girl whose idyllic world was shattered. Through her pain, she came to discover the love of a Father she'd never met before.

Through unimaginable loss, Brenda and her sister grew up with their widowed mother, who, at times, didn't know where their next meal was coming from. Brenda was exposed to predators who took advantage of her vulnerability at a perilously young age. The ensuing damage impacted Brenda so severely that the forces of rage surfaced in her while darkness and hate slept in her bed every night.

The darkness subsided for the first time when her mother, Sherry Epperson, gave Brenda her first personalized Bible. Her thirst for hope and truth was so gargantuan that as she turned each page, a revelation took place. For the first time, she recognized that God's love was greater than any pain she had ever faced and would ever face in the future. It was the lightning bolt realization that she didn't have to fight her battles alone anymore. Through this awakening, Brenda visualized herself helping others in distant lands while accomplishing feats that she could never have imagined.

Acknowledgements

THEY SAY IT TAKES a village, and that is what it took for me to complete this book; therefore, I would like to thank and acknowledge my family and friends who prayed, helped, and inspired me to keep writing, all the while strengthening me with their unconditional love and friendship, which gave me the ability to finish this book. Thank you to my mother, whose prayers have always guided me, and to my precious recently departed father, who is no doubt laughing and dancing in heaven. My sister Deborah, we always have each other's back, and my dear friend and (sister) Dena. Deanna, Isik, and Zoro who constantly said, "You can do this." A gratitude of thanks to Diana Addison-Lyle for getting me over the hump.

Special thanks to Cindy Tait and Shelley Anderson Myers, who made me laugh when I cried and simply would not let me quit. You were the constant wall of words, love, and ideas I needed to finish this project. Your friendship is invaluable to me. Love you all so much!

Joy

1

Joy In Pain

God works good in all things for those who love him
and are called according to His purpose.

—ROMANS 8:28 NIV

A FEW YEARS AGO, my car was broken into. The front driver's side window was completely smashed in. The thieves had grabbed my favorite purse, which I hid under some articles of clothing. As I heard my alarm sound, I ran towards my car, only to be greeted by my shattered window. My *joy* evaporated instantly, along with the crumbling window of my car.

At that moment I noticed my cell phone peeping out from the side of the car; God had mercifully hidden it from the thief's sight. I called out to my daughters protectively—corralling them so I knew they were safe. As their little feet scampered towards me, what impacted my mind most was how much worse this could have been. I'd already mentally calculated that the thieves had scouted the area beforehand, surveying the most lucrative potential: a mom with her young daughters was a soft target. Confirming their first impressions of us, they watched our parking, and when I walked away from the car without my purse, they probably determined that this would be the perfect car to hit. It's an uneasy realization to know that thieves are surveying your every move—just like about-to-pounce predators. Mercifully, they hit the car without us there, or this could have become a violent situation if we intercepted the theft.

We retrieved what the thieves left behind: our hidden cell phones, and with that, I could begin damage control by calling our credit card companies to cancel the cards immediately. My instinct was to remedy a bad situation by minimizing potential damage.

By the time the police arrived to take the report, I felt a sense of measurable relief. That's usually when tears begin to cascade, but I fought back the waterworks because it would have interfered with the next steps. The shattered window was a stark reminder of the violation of our personal space and a sense of loss. But it was more than that. The thieves stole sensitive information including my ID, recently-withdrawn hard cash, a favorite purse, and a brand-new wallet that my husband and daughters had bought me for Mother's Day. Also stolen was my deacon badge from the church. I reflected on all the many things that were stolen and kept coming back to that deacon badge. I have to admit, I was secretly hoping the thieves would see that badge and be instantly convicted to return the purse, along with my money, credit cards, and belongings.

Aware that my daughters were now studying my every move, I determined to make the choice to hold my peace. Was I going to completely fall apart or trust God and show my children that God *does* work good in all things? So, I quietly prayed, did what I needed to do, held my peace with God's strength, and remained kind.

When the police had completed their report, they inquired how I planned to drive home with broken glass on the seats. Grace was immediately shown when the kind officers began cleaning out all the glass so that I could leave the scene of the crime without the prospect of glass cutting into us on the way home. One of the officers even cut his hand while pulling large chunks of splintered glass hanging from my windshield. We were effectively saved from that loose, razor-edged chunk that could have sliced into one of us as we drove the car on the freeway—back to the place where we felt safe. I recognized that the officer's act of kindness, which went above the call of duty, had prevented a potentially hazardous drive home.

The next day I took my car to the dealership. The technician told me he couldn't help me because this particular window had to be specially ordered for the glass, and that would take weeks. Mini miracle number one occurred when he paused, looked again at his computer, and said, "I actually have one sitting in the back and it's cheaper. It will save you about $150." I thought, "Glory hallelujah!"

I then began to share my story with the technician, explaining the details of the smash-and-grab, and instead of being angry, I found myself praying for the men who broke into my car. I began to share how I wanted to be quick to forgive and slow to anger, which I admit is still a work in progress. He listened, whole-heartedly agreed, and thanked me for sharing my story. Then he said something that struck me: "We all make mistakes." As he hung his head low, I recognized that his comment was, perhaps, loaded with meaning, but I did not want to pry into something that he might not be willing to share.

Later in the day, the technician called me to tell me my car was done, and he said proudly, "Guess what? I saved you $200 in total." The small blessings were pouring in, and looking back, I often wonder if the same outcome would have happened had I walked into that service station filled with anger instead of faith. I learned later that the technician who saved me all that money had been a troubled young man at one time. The story I shared with him struck a chord because he went out of his way to help me. This was a man who—in his past—had not always done the right thing. I'd like to think that the kindness he displayed was a response to the grace that was at one time shown to him.

Looking back, I realize that at the scene of the crime, I made a conscious decision to remain in *joy* even though my circumstances were not lining up. I'm not sure the outcome would have been the same with the officers *or* the car technician if I had approached everything in anger and accusation instead of *joy*. There is a saying that goes something like this: "Every action has an equal and opposite reaction." I've learned in life that people aren't as willing to help when I'm angry.

> Pleasant words are a honeycomb sweet to the soul and healing to the bones. (Proverbs 16:24 NKJV)

Being quick to forgive allows us to walk and flow in love, grace, *joy*, and mercy, which I believe causes others to want to help us. I've seen it, I believe it, and I've lived it!

Joy is a state of mind and an orientation of the heart. It is a settled state of contentment, confidence, and hope. It is something or someone that provides a source of happiness. *Joy* is different from happiness. Happiness is a temporary emotion, while *joy* is a state of mind, a decision.

I AM

Jesus

On

You

What does that mean, *Jesus On You?* Three letters are used to make the word *joy*. The number three is significant in scripture and often signifies a marked event within scripture with over four hundred references to the number. Often God is referred to as the God of Abraham, Isaac, and Jacob—three significant figures in the Hebrew Bible, also known as the three patriarchs. The three righteous patriarchs before the flood were Noah, Enoch, and Abel. Genesis 1:3 states, "And God said, Let there be light: and there was light" (NIV). Jonah spent three days in the belly of the great fish. Jesus prayed three times in the Garden of Gethsemane before his arrest, and after being crucified, he rose on the third day. Jesus was placed on the cross the third hour of the day; three hours of darkness came over the land while Jesus suffered on the cross. Then, there is the Blessed Holy Trinity of God the Father, God the Son, and God the Holy Spirit.

Why *joy?* According to Psalm 43:4, *Joy* is *not* because of what God gives to us (our situations, etc.), but because of *who He* is. *Joy* is the very essence of who God is. True *JOY* can only be found in Jesus and through Jesus, while and when He is (the great I AM) JESUS ON YOU. #IJOY

It's like when we wear our favorite fragrance, a sweet aroma that we put *on* us:

> For we are to God the sweet aroma of Christ among those who are being saved and those who are perishing. For we are a sweet perfume to God. (2 Corinthians 2:15 BSB)

When Jesus is on us and in us, He doesn't see us in our sin and guilt. We are covered in beauty, forgiven, shameless, drenched in a beautiful fragrance.

Like a fragrance, when Jesus is on you, the *JOY* that simply exists in him exists and *rests* on you. This is one of the many attributes of Jesus. The great, I AM *JOY*, is then on you and me! As Christians, we should be saturated with the aroma of *JOY* just like a fine perfume. That aroma or fragrance causes others to pause and take notice. It's like when you are wearing perfume or cologne and a stranger stops you and asks, "What are you wearing? It smells so good." This fragrance draws that person to you and creates an inviting opportunity to talk, share, and connect.

Having *joy*, or I*JOY*, is the fruit of the spirit. When we have *joy* in us we can look at and tackle problems and circumstances with a victor's outlook rather than a defeated or critical perspective. When we are saturated with I*JOY*, we live and walk in a fullness of abundance that is engaging and inviting to others. This *joy* causes others to respond. It draws them to us and at times creates a desire in them to want to help us and do things for us beyond their job description. The technician who helped me with my broken window and the policemen who cleaned the broken glass out of my car showed me kindness and grace over and above what was required.

> Consider it pure *joy*, my brothers and sisters, whenever you face
> trials of many kinds, because you know that the testing of your
> faith produces perseverance. (James 1:2–3 NIV)

Joy appears eighty-eight times in the Hebrew Bible, in twenty-two books, and fifty-seven times in the New Testament, in eighteen books (according to Theopedia).[1] Paul mentions some of the fruits of the spirit to be love, *joy*, peace, patience, kindness, goodness, gentleness, self-control, and faithfulness. Just like natural fruit trees need water to stay sweet-tasting and inviting and pleasing to eat, so do we. As we draw closer to God, He cuts the weeds in our lives and waters us as we read the word and develop these fruits in our daily walk with Him.

It seems to me that there is a decline in *joy* with people today. This was never more apparent when one day I stood in a long line at Coffee Bean. Minding my own business, I heard God's voice in my right ear say, "Buy that woman a cup of coffee." She was standing right in front of me. I could only see her from behind. So, the dialog began in my spirit. I replied in my heart, "What?" Gently, the same voice, "Buy that woman a cup of coffee." I know the voice of God in my heart, so I thought, "Okay, yes, I will, no problem." As we neared the front counter I stuck out my cash and said, "Here, it's on me," in a hushed tone. What happened next was *not* the reaction I had expected. This woman turned around, shot me a look, and then began yelling loudly, at me. As her voice raised even higher, she screamed, "What do you think you are doing? I can buy my cup of coffee! How dare you!" Shocked, I quickly told her I was so sorry for offending her, and I was just trying to do something nice. I was trying to pour water on a very explosive situation by expressing my apologies—explaining that I had no ill intention other than to be kind. I was horrified and told her once again I was sorry if I offended her. She responded with a terse, "I don't need it," and walked away indignantly.

1. https://www.theopedia.com/joy.

I was mortified that I had offended her, but interestingly, she didn't stop the transaction from being made. By this time, the cashier was even giving me a dirty look as the line grew out the door. I was reduced to a meek version of my former self, and I muttered underneath my breath, "I'll have a cup of coffee . . . with a shot of espresso." The cashier rolled his eyes as he took my money for both our drinks while I contemplated where to stand so that I would not deliver any more offensive gestures. I had no choice but to enter the "drinks pickup line" and stood nervously behind the lady I had so clearly insulted. I dared not look at the people behind me as the cashier's dirty looks and heavy sighs were enough humiliation for one day.

Confusion reigned in my head as I wrestled with God, asking Him how I could have been so wrong when His voice had sounded so clear to me. "Did I hear you incorrectly, Lord? What should I have done differently?" A succession of apologies to God followed before I was stopped in my tracks by the same lady whose heart appeared to have been touched. As tears welled up in her eyes, she turned to me and said, "Why did you buy *me* a cup of coffee?" Afraid of being yelled at again, and unsure of the right answer, I simply said, "I don't know. I just wanted to bless you . . . to do something nice." She looked at me intently, and as tears began to pour down her face she said, "Nobody ever does anything this nice for me. Nobody has ever done something like this for me. Thank you."

I was speechless. I became choked up and all I could say was, "God bless you." She paused, we exchanged a beautiful moment, and she took her coffee and left. I never saw her again. I don't know her name or anything about her, but God does. I will never know what happened to the lady, but what I do know for certain is that, in our dramatic little encounter, God had a purpose for her. I have come to realize that even the smallest act of love or kindness can make *huge* and dramatic impacts on other people's lives. It was so clear this poor lady lacked *joy*. God used that small interaction to give her back something she had lost.

Perhaps that small act gave her a moment of *joy*, love, and acceptance. Perhaps she had just lost a loved one. Maybe she had just lost her job and was scared of how she was going to survive and pay her bills. Perhaps she was contemplating on ending her life. I don't know, but I *do* know that when we do seemingly insignificant small things for others, it not only brings *joy* to them but also blesses our own lives. I will never forget her, and I will never stop doing small, and big things, for others.

The smash-and-grab car break-in, as well as the incident of buying a cup of coffee for the lady, clearly showed that even when things go radically wrong in life, staying in grace, preserving the peace, trusting God, and keeping our *joy* allows God to do His work louder than any of our screaming or angry words.

> Not all of us can do great things. But we can do small things with great love. (Mother Teresa)

There are many different kinds of *joy*. In Greek, *chara*, or in Latin, *gaudium*; *joy* is deeper than mere happiness, it is rooted in God and comes from Him. Since it comes from God, it is more stable than worldly happiness, which is merely emotional and temporary. Happiness can be a fleeting moment, whereas *joy*, God's *joy*, becomes a part of us. Paul writes,

> Rejoice in the Lord always again I say rejoice.
> (Philippians 4:4 NIV)

Rejoice in the Lord. Not in our circumstances, but in the Lord. That's not to make light of our circumstances that are challenging or difficult but to remind us that our eyes need to stay fixed on Him. Having a victor's perspective causes our *joy* to rise, which then gives us strength.

Another incident that is a good illustration of the choices we have the power to make took place on a family vacation years ago in Hawaii. To me, Hawaii is one of the most beautiful, relaxing places on earth. It brings me peace as I watch each of my family members leave behind the worries of their daily reality as they cast their cares and concerns to the Hawaiian breeze. For my family, it's one of the most perfect places for healthy detoxification.

We were on the beach on an idyllic Hawaiian island day. The weather could not have been more perfect, the sand any cooler, or the aqua waves more resplendent. Once my family had set up our chairs in the sand, our beach towels tucked neatly on each chair, we sat down, exhaling completely. I had my book in hand and a thirst-quenching drink next to me when, suddenly, one of my young daughters accidentally spilled my husband's drink everywhere. Let me preface this by saying that my husband is typically the best-natured man I know. He is slow to anger and rich in kindness. His natural disposition is to be exceptionally calm during these types of situations, but for some reason, he became angry and started yelling loudly. Our serene beach scene with its quiet waves and peaceful tranquility was suspended. It was paradise lost! Concerned that people were disturbed by our situation, I gently said, "Honey, quiet." This only aggravated the situation, and chaos ensued as my husband ranted on a bit more to our visibly upset daughters. Our peaceful haven was shattered. Feeling *joy* was not the first thing to pop into my mind, but God has always protected my heart and I said loudly, "I am happy! I'm en*joy*ing my day, and nothing anyone does is going to change that!" The couple behind us began to laugh, and I turned to them with a big smile on my face and said, "Are you with me?" They laughed again and *joy*ously said "Yes!"

Silence fell over my family, and I knelt down and began to help clean up the mess. Sometimes you have to hold your angry tongue and proclaim *joy*. I call it "loud *JOY*." Sometimes you have to proclaim your *joy* loudly, shout it from the rooftop.

> The *joy* of the Lord is your strength. (Nehemiah 8:10 NIV)

The fruit of the spirit of *joy*, is the understanding that God is ultimately in control. *He* is sovereign.

> God is our refuge and strength, an ever-present help in times of trouble. (Psalm 46:1 NIV)

This type of *JOY* IS *JESUS ON YOU*, it's the type of *IJOY* which is attractive, makes us more attractive, and ultimately points others towards Jesus. We know the source of our *joy* is the great I AM, which is, Jesus On You.

JESUS—HOLY SPIRIT—GOD YAHWEH *J O Y*

JESUS—Is in us and on us forever when we invite him into our hearts.

HOLY SPIRIT—is a complete circle. When Jesus ascended into heaven he sent the Holy Spirit, the great comforter, to be *on you* with an *unquenchable fire*. In Genesis, the Bible says, "The Holy Spirit was hovering over all the earth" (Gen 1:2 NIV). *IJOY* is hovering over you and is *in* you and *on* you because our heavenly father is in us and on us; will you accept the Holy Spirit's invitation? Fire communicates the very essence or presence of GOD and/or the Holy Spirit. This unquenchable fire is *on me,* and remains on me and in me, through trials, struggles, deep sorrow, and pain. Because of this, we are all able to survive and thrive during some of life's most painful and difficult situations.

God (Yahweh)—Is the great I AM.

IJOY—I AM Jesus On You

You see, as a young girl, I didn't realize that our *joy* comes from the Lord. Did you know it's our birthright? It's one of over three thousand promises that are in the Bible from God himself—a gift that each one of us has when we are born on this earth. Perhaps you, like myself at times, have completely lost your *joy* because of circumstances, illness, heartache, injustice, loss, or just plain life. God promises to be your exceeding *joy*.

Have you ever noticed or stopped to ponder on the fact that God often speaks to us through the gentle, simple, and the obvious? Oftentimes, we are waiting for the earthquake, lightning, or thunderous voice from above. I have found in my own life more often than not, it's the still, small voice that has the most impact or makes the most difference in and through my life. I have learned to find *joy* in the simple and seemingly mundane things in life. So often I find myself running around so much looking for the big things that I miss the small things, which, in my opinion, are the foundation for the larger triumphs and victories we en*joy*—all of which build and increase our own *joy*.

Joy is found usually in a situation, a moment, or even a physical reaction. What this book is about is how to use what God has given you and what life sometimes hands you, and make a conscious decision to *Rise Up* in *joy* anyway, even in the midst of the blowing storm. It's about Jesus On You, which is a gift of everlasting *JOY—IJOY* that will cause us to *Rise Up* and can be found even when life throws us a curveball or at times when the experience or situations of life are contradictory to the situation.

Prayer

Heavenly Father I ask that you increase *joy* over us, overwhelm us with your love, give us new courage and boldness to be kind to strangers. Shatter wrong ideas about ourselves and others, and bind the lies of the enemy. I decree a new breakthrough authority over you as you allow God to sanctify you, set you apart, fill you with a new heavenly *joy*, and use your life so God's love will be poured out into others in Jesus' name.

Challenge Questions

1. What is one goal you can set today to increase your *joy*?

2. What is one thing you can do for someone else to bring *them joy*?

3. How will a deeper walk with Jesus strengthen your *joy*?

4. What can you do today to redirect your mind from fear to *joy*?

2

Childhood Interrupted

Life and death are in the tongue.
—*PROVERBS 18:21 BSB*

I GREW UP IN a fun-loving household with my father, Don, mother, Sherry, and older sister, Deborah. My dad was the central fountain of energy in our home and with that energy came lots of laughter—which suited me perfectly. Laughter permeated every fiber of my being. I'd throw my head back, laughing loudly and often. I remember people always saying, "Shhhhh, Brenda you are being too loud . . . Brenda, quit laughing." Admittedly, the church was probably not the best place to do it. A friend of mine once described me as being the Fourth of July, every day, all day long.

My mother gave me a book as a young girl that shaped my ideas of life. The author was Anne Keimel, and the book was called "I'm out to Change my World." After digesting the entire book, I felt a new sense of purpose and clarity, that with a big God, small things become giant in His hands. This new thought was so incredibly exciting to me. As it grew in my spirit, my mind expanded.

Don Epperson, my dad, inhabited a room like nobody I have ever known. My starry eyes were fixated on him as he lit up every room with his larger-than-life presence. His musical gift was legendary, and I'd sit at his feet mesmerized as he pored over his sheet music, composing new melodies on the lucky guitar—the one that traveled with him around the United States. The happiness I felt during those evenings was immeasurably comforting. I felt warm, safe, uplifted, and deeply loved. It was during those years that Dad's music permeated my soul, inhabiting every inch of my being. Our family wasn't perfect, but through my young eyes, it was pretty close. Life was full with a loving family and everything a child needs or dreams of having.

Dad's successes moved him around the USA as he charted two top-10 hits while signed with Capital RCA/Capital Victor. He was also known for his co-starring role with western legend John Wayne in the feature film, *Big Jake*. My mother, a costume designer who studied under her idol, the famous Edith Head, would work feverishly on creating my father's next unique stage outfit while my sister and I rolled around on the ground—on all of the fabric pieces launched from my mom's massive sewing table.

I was a bit of a tomboy growing up, while my older sister played with her Barbie dolls and campers, I had remote control race cars. I loved climbing on the trees with the neighborhood boys. I remember dirt biking and roughhousing with the boys. I found very little interest in Barbie in those days. Mom would often make me sit down as she would strongly comb through my hair while I screamed, "That hurts!" to which she would reply, "It wouldn't hurt if you would brush your hair once in a while instead of climbing trees. Now sit still!" She was right; the beauty or look of my hair was the last thing on my mind.

Just when my young life appeared to be on track, a regular good night's sleep was interrupted by a tragedy my family could never have anticipated. As my sister and I had skipped off to bed, we expected to wake up with the Californian sun and our family life safely intact. Instead, I awoke to hear what sounded like a desperate seal howling in the dark. Alarmed, we jumped out of our bunk beds and inched our way down the patchwork floor that dad had created. The cruelty of what I saw as we entered the livingroom would be seared in my memory forever. Barely able to breathe, mom mustered every ounce of energy left in her to pull her face away from her hands in order to deliver to us the piercingly painful words, "Your father has gone to heaven." I blacked out when I heard the words that were impossible to absorb, and the next thing I remember was being on the lap of my neighbor's embrace, sobbing hysterically.

My father had just left us the day before to shoot a movie in Mexico, and on his way to the film location, his car flew off a cliff, throwing him from the vehicle. He was killed instantly.

I was seven years old. In one five-minute stroke of fate, we lost the father we loved deeply and the rock that we thought would always be there to protect us. My dad was only thirty-two years old. His death was shattering. My mom became an instant young widow whose emotional loss was so devastating that waking up the next day seemed like an insurmountable task. My sister and I became semi orphans with no handbook on how to negotiate our life or our grief. All we could do was follow our instincts, which took us down a path of utilizing various survival mechanisms that were not necessarily healthy. My ten-year-old sister became an overly conscientious protector while my seven-year-old instincts prodded me even more towards rough-housing with other children—mostly boys. It was the only way I knew how to let out the surging emotions inside of me. Much of that time is blurred in my memory as I navigated through the different phases of shock. What I do remember clearly is that I became progressively more angry at the devastating turn in my life.

Sometime later while walking down to the neighbor's house, I remember looking up into the heavens at God, shaking my fists, and saying three words that I now regret: "I hate you, God." Just writing those words now puts a chill down my spine. I was broken, tormented, and grief-stricken. All the laughter and all my *joy* had disappeared—stolen in the blink of an eye.

My family and I attended a Lutheran Church not far from my home in the San Fernando Valley. Growing up I always knew about Jesus. He was the guy in the pictures with the white robe who seemed to really like sheep and children . . . a lot. This was comforting to me because I also liked sheep a lot. I also remember—from pictures—that this Jesus guy always had a smile on his face when he was around kids, which was another comforting realization during my childhood years.

In our small church, the children were often invited to come up to the front of the church to recite the weekly verse from memory. We didn't have cue cards or cheat sheets, just the good brains God gave us. Each week the Sunday school teacher would pass out the verses and the children would read their verses out loud as she handed them out. I remember hearing things such as, "God is love," or "Love your neighbor as yourself."

One week, I anticipated getting my verse. When the Sunday school teacher handed it to me, I was shocked down to my toes. I looked at my page, back at her, and at my page again. It certainly had to be a mistake. I raised my hand and tentatively stated, "This is way too long, I can't do this." She just smiled and said, "Oh, yes you can," and without skipping a beat, kept on passing out the note cards to the other children. I thought she must have been crazy. Or was she? Then I thought, maybe she saw something in me that I didn't quite see in myself yet. The passage she gave me to read was one I would still quote to this day, the Great Commission:

> And Jesus came and said to them, 'All authority in heaven and on earth has been given me. Go, therefore, and make disciples of all nations, baptizing them in the name of the Father, and of the Son, and of the Holy Spirit, teaching them to observe all that I have commanded you. And behold, I am with you always, to the end of the age. (Matthew 28: 18–20 ESV)

Through much time and hard work, I finally memorized this verse, and it resonated deeply within my soul. It would be many years later that this verse would make such an impact in my life and be the cornerstone of my lifetime Christian outreach. I would come to realize that God made *no* mistake in having my Sunday school teacher hand me that memory verse so many years ago. It was divine, and it was purposed.

My life as I knew it was over for many reasons. Just before my father's death, my parents decided to cancel all my dad's insurance policies, so financial hardship mounted on top of my mother's grief. Even though my mother tried, she had no way to support the vast bills we had and raise two daughters on her own. She turned the garage into a studio and began sewing and designing clothes for people, but she could not maintain the heavy financial responsibilities. Forced by circumstances, my mother sold everything we had, including our house.

School became a challenge and my grades suffered terribly. I made frequent trips to the principal's office and was constantly getting into fights with other girls and boys. Basically, I would fight with anyone who made me feel worse than I already felt. In second grade, I was known as the "angry girl" or "the girl with whom not to mess," because I would immediately lash out and start a physical fight with anyone who made fun of me. One time in second grade, a fight with my classmate was so severe that we both had fistfuls of each other's hair and beet-red faces from squeezing, scratching, and grabbing. Her cruel words, "I'm glad your dad is dead," provoked the attack. My future was not looking very promising at this tender age as back to the principal's office I went.

In desperation, my mother packed our family of three and moved us to Winnemucca, Nevada, to live with her sister and their family. Things became even worse. I had spiraled downward from being a happy, *joyful* child, into a deeply troubled little girl filled with anger and a knee-jerk reaction to the things I couldn't control. I was utterly and completely lost.

Looking back, I realize that in the awful moment when I yelled out the three terrible words to God, "I hate you," something shifted in me, and I believe that it opened a door for Satan to begin placing a stronghold of bitterness and anger in my life and heart which led to my downward spiral. My anger overwhelmed me as I railed at the injustices of life. Many people knew that my father had died, but many people did not know a secret I carried around. Shortly before my father died, something evil happened to me, and no one knew.

My family was very social; we always had block parties and people over at our house. One day, while our neighbors visited, I went into the house to watch television, and a boy from the neighborhood came into the house as well. We played hide-and-seek, and as I hid behind my father's chair, he came up on me and raped me. I was only six years old and cried out for him to stop, but he didn't listen and continued to forcibly violate me. I don't remember what happened after that as the shock has a way of shutting down our memories—especially when our brains can't compute the enormity of the situation. All I knew was that something very bad and wrong had happened to me. My heart cried out with pain, in silence, suffering, and my burgeoning anger escalated out of control on that dark day. No child should ever encounter what I had to face.

My grades suffered tremendously in unison with my emotional devastation. I continued to get into fights at school while anger became my destructive ally, my outlet for emotions that I didn't understand. My *joy* had been shattered and so began the internal struggle for power over my very soul. To my detriment, I wasn't afraid of anybody or anything anymore. The part I didn't understand, though, was that as my anger intensified, my sadness grew unimaginably deeper every day. It was like a lethal mixture: anger fueled my sadness and sadness fueled my anger. I was so lost and misguided that I figured that when I felt deflated or defeated, a good fight or a fit of rage would make it all go away. I thought that my punching routine gave me strength, but in reality, I was becoming increasingly more exhausted, weak, more troubled, angry, and completely isolated. It was a vicious cycle in which I was feeding the monstrous anger I was trying to control. That was the moment where I felt I needed to reduce the fighting and challenge people less but that didn't work either. I felt afraid, alone, ganged-up-on, insecure, ugly, fat, confused, and betrayed. While my mother and sister showed me constant, unconditional love, at home, my heart was aching, and the daily sadness replaced all my *joy*.

My heart was dying, my *joy* was dying, our dog suddenly died, the cat ran away, and even our ducks had drowned. Death surrounded me like a sandstorm with no visibility in sight.

My mom's loneliness grew. Often, I would walk in her room and find her crying at the edge of her bed. When I would ask what was wrong, she would try to reassure me that everything was all right, but I knew her look of sadness too well. Sometimes she would say, "I miss your father," and sometimes she would say, "I'm worried about paying the bills." As much as she tried to shield us from all that was going on, my heart ached for her, and as a little girl, there was nothing I could do to ease her fears or her pain. The three of us all felt it and there was no solution in sight, the only way out would be through a miracle by God's miraculous hand.

After we moved to Nevada, my mom met a man who seemed to put a huge smile back onto her face. He was tall, a cowboy kind of guy, and very funny. We would all spend time together, and it seemed as though my mom had finally found love again. I would later discover that my mother, like all of us, was facing insecurities in her life. She didn't feel as though she was strong enough, or capable of managing an entire household while raising two girls on her own.

In hindsight and knowing what I know now, I realize that oftentimes we are stronger than we realize, but we lose sight of that strength when something, or someone, presents itself as being easier. My mom thought she could make it work and learn to love this man in order to have security for us all. My mom ended up marrying this man, and we moved to the middle of nowhere with our new stepfather and his two children.

I remember the place vividly. It was a double-wide trailer home in the desert with no sight of human life within the eye's distance. We would have to search for miles for any sign of people. I remember my sister and I would entertain ourselves for hours by running through the small bodies of water that would accumulate after the rains. We would catch tadpoles and chase our dogs with all our excess energy. However, what I thought might turn out to be an idyllic life took a turn for the worst.

Things began to escalate out of control as this new man in our lives had a horrible drinking problem and temper, and nine times out of ten, he was drunk. Added to that, his daughter and I began to butt heads on a daily basis.

18

I am not perfect by any stretch of the imagination, but this girl had a cunning way of turning everything around and putting the blame on me. For example, if a dish broke, she said I did it. If chores weren't done, she said it was my turn. She even went as far as to make up lies that I was calling her names and stealing, when in fact, that is what she was doing to me. I would tell her dad I wasn't doing any of that, but he never believed me. The rage that came out of him scared me enormously. The strife in the house began to escalate; my mother went from happy to constant tears. Fear began to grip my heart as his daughter relentlessly tried to crush me. One day a fight broke out between my mom and stepfather, and it was apparently the straw that broke the camel's back. My stepfather stormed out and threatened that when he got back, a spanking was in order. That spanking would clearly be for me. My mom tried her best to stand in the way of him, and my sister and I, but things had escalated to a violent level. I felt horrible that I had caused all of this to happen and blamed myself for my mother feeling the way she did. I felt I had somehow let her down horribly and stolen her *joy* away. I had this little problem of not being able to keep my mouth shut, and that definitely escalated things. I felt unjustly criticized and blamed for everything this girl had done to me, and I was tired of always trying to defend myself against actions that I had not caused. Once again, I felt despair, sadness, and betrayal.

Apparently, after that huge blow-up, my mom called my aunt and uncle and asked if we could move back in with them again. She feared physical abuse, probably for us all. Somehow my mom devised a plan that we were going to the laundromat to wash our clothes, when in fact, the only clothes and shoes she loaded were our own. She carefully loaded the laundry bags with all of our belongings, careful to disguise anything other than laundry. Of course, we never went to the laundromat. We simply drove to my aunt and uncle's house for safety and never looked back. I remember feeling a sense of relief as we escaped the unknown terrors of what might have become part of our lives.

That two-month marriage ended abruptly. I felt safe again living with my Aunt Joey, Uncle Ron, and two cousins. There was a lot of laughter in the house. They had horses and chickens on a small farm, and there was always lots to do. While making friends at school was almost impossible, I always looked forward to coming home to be with my family, and all of the animals in our home. They brought me a sense of stability and security as our daily routines began to smooth out the fears and pain of the past.

My aunt and her family regularly attended a Pentecostal church, a place where they worshiped God differently and expressed themselves with openness and freedom. I was in awe of the uninhibited worship of a people that sang, praised, and prayed in a way that I had never seen before. One evening at a candle-lit service, each of us held candles while the pastor preached. Suddenly, I felt a kind of love that overwhelmed my soul and spirit. It was as though the battle that raged on in my heart and soul was coming to an end. That night at the tender age of nine, while in my Uncle Ron's arms, holding a candle tears streaming down my face, I accepted Christ into my heart.

It was like an electric bolt of lightning, the shock of love surged through my body, and I was free! Immediately, I felt *joy* again and a deep love wrapped around me as I had never known before. Three words rang through my heart and spirit, "I Love You." There it was . . . three words again. My *joy* had been restored, the grip of anger melted away, and I felt the smile on my face as God's immeasurable, indescribable love wrapped around my heart, mind, body, and soul. *Joy* was brought back to me by Him.

I understand there are different types of healing. Sometimes, we are healed and delivered by God with a rapid Divine Healing; suddenly, all at once, we are released from fear and bondage or physical pain. While other times, healing can be a slower process; the scars are still there, but God, in His magnificent wisdom and grace, draws a new beautiful painting over the scars of bondage and creates a new destiny for us, and through our suffering, creates an artwork that is an awe-inspiring display of the stupendous power of God almighty. This was one such day for me in my young heart.

> If I did anything right in my life, it was when I gave my heart to you. (unknown)

Oh, how I am eternally grateful for those pastors in small communities, who then and now, faithfully week after week, preach and profess the truth of God and proclaim the good news!

Soon after, feeling the power and overwhelming love of God, I began to crave the word of God. I had an insatiable desire to read my Bible almost every day, I actually wanted to go to church and began to envision myself in faraway lands helping people I did not know and had never even seen.

My dreams began before the internet, so they were derived from a map and my imagination. I was only nine, and coming from where I had been emotionally, this was truly a miracle that could only have come from

God. This is what is called child-like faith. While I was still a child at nine, being reborn with the heart of Christ in me gave me what I call a "foolish faith." I figured if God can do anything, and He's on the inside of me, then so can I. I would finally begin to see myself as God saw me—limitless.

> I can do all things through Christ who strengthens me.
> (Philippians 4:13 NKJV)

Jesus Christ is limitless, and he dwells inside of our soul and in our hearts, which gives us access to unlimited possibilities—where the impossible becomes possible.

> I'd rather ask God for everything and get some of it, instead of asking God for nothing and getting all of it. (Joyce Meyer)

Research shows that babies will start reflex smiling as soon as they are born, and they will even smile in their sleep. Accordingly, experts at Baylor College of Medicine (BCM) wrote an article in *Science Daily* about a smile lighting up the reward centers of our brain.

Researchers hooked up twenty-eight moms to a machine to scan their brain blood flow while showing them pictures of babies or kids smiling. Upon seeing a picture of a smiling child, the frontal lobe—which involves emotion and motor behavioral outputs—was activated.

According to Dr. Lane Stratharn, assistant professor of pediatrics at BCM Texas Children's Hospital, and a research associate in BCM's Human Neuroimaging Laboratory, "These are areas that have been activated in other experiments associated with drug addiction." He goes on to say, "It may be that seeing your own baby's smiling face is like a 'natural high.'"[1]

Wouldn't it be amazing if all of us took the time to smile more so others could feel a constant natural high? We would all feel more loved, more accepted, and more welcomed. My mom used to tell me that when she woke me up, a smile was the first expression my face made.

I guess you could say I was born with *joy*, but aren't all babies? I was born with *joy* and so were you.

A well-known evangelist was talking about a doctor he knew and a patient of this doctor. Every time she would come into his office, she would talk about how sick she was or her medical condition. One time, instead of prescribing more medicine, the doctor prescribed her something unusual. He said, "I am writing you a prescription for *joy*. You must go home and

---

1. Baylor College of Medicine, "Baby's Smile."

for 3–4 weeks, everyday speak the words, "I am happy, I am healthy, I am whole, on and on." When she arrived back in his office a while later, many of her ailments were gone. *Joy* is so powerful! Did you know the Bible talks about the fact that each one of us has an angel assigned to us? That gives me *joy* just thinking about the power behind that.

What if there was an angel with you every day with armloads of gifts, custom-made for you, but you refused to accept them because you couldn't see them? Life often chokes out our *joy* and ability to see or accept the gifts God has waiting for us. The fact is, there *are* angels standing by you right now, waiting to unlock the secret places and treasures that you don't know are there. Will you receive them? They are a free gift. I invite you today to say *yes*!

> Are not all angels ministering spirits sent to serve those who will inherit salvation? (Hebrews 1:14 NIV)

Prayer

Dear Lord unchain my mind, dismantle the strongholds that would weigh me down and cause me to sink. Replace the lukewarmness in my life with the fire of God and the power of the Holy Spirit. Calm the turbulent waters around me and in me, so I can *Rise Up*, into the calling you have for my life.

Challenge Questions

1. Identify three things that may be holding you back from experiencing *joy*.

2. What is one thing you can do to change your thought life about *joy*?

3. Will you commit yourself to smile, wave, say hello, or give a compliment to a complete stranger today? Write YES and make a difference in someone's life.

3

Breaking into Mercy

WE CONTINUED TO GO to the same church where I gave my life to Christ, but then life took another turn. We moved from Winnemucca, Nevada, to a small logging town called Dallas, Oregon, with a population of six thousand. This was quite a departure from the cities I was used to. We found a beautiful church and attended services regularly. My grade school years didn't lighten up, and it didn't take me long to experience full-scale rejection in our new town and culture. I became a prime target for bullying before the word was used for kids beating up on other kids.

My father's untimely death, coupled with the terrible secret I carried of being raped as a child, created a deep sadness that took over my heart and soul. A broken heart manifests itself in various ways: in my case, I ate to feed my fractured heart, and it didn't generate a healthy result. My weight gain elicited every cruel name related to fat. The relentless, merciless teasing by other kids at school was delivered to me emotionally and physically on a daily basis. The physical abuse took many turns including being pushed off swings while I was in midair, being "accidentally" pushed or tripped in the hallway of the school. A particularly humiliating event seared in my memory was being spit on by two boys as I walked home with my friend one day while being called fat and ugly and all sorts of other disgusting names. My *joy* seemed to be slipping further and further away as I sunk to an all-time low with feelings of worthlessness and pain.

Through it all, God's divine strength never left me. Despite the challenges, *joy* etched itself slowly back into my life, allowing the girl I used to be to surface again. I would find small glimpses of laughter and the smile that seemed to have vacated my face returned.

During this time, I discovered the *joy* of working with animals. In our small community, I began to volunteer my time after school and on weekends on a farm and as a veterinarian's helper. Both of these opportunities brought me so much *joy* because animals gave me unconditional acceptance and care without judgment. My sister and I would immerse ourselves for hours at the farm, and we relished being there. I would laugh heartily with the animals, especially with my adoptive little goat, Patches, and my bull, Bully.

I would often reflect and remember the look on Jesus' face in those pictures I saw when I was a little girl. My thought processes finally understood why Jesus liked animals so much. They brought nothing but *joy*. I translated that to my experience: the animals didn't care what I looked like, or how much I weighed, or whether or not I was able to afford designer clothes. There were no conditions attached to their loving me. Working on that blissful farm drew me closer to Jesus. I understood how He sees our hearts on the inside, not the outward adornment. Milestones of achievement and progress were etched daily as I taught my bull, Bully, and goat, Patches, to come to me when I called on command. Seeing that my life had an impact gave me confidence and strength and also helped with a much-needed escape from the bullying I received from kids at school. Rejection damages our self-esteem, causes us to feel unloved or unwanted, or like we don't belong, but in the kingdom of God, you always belong.

> God judges not so much the outside as He does the inside. He looks to the motives, thoughts, and intentions of your heart.
> (Billy Graham)

Through it all, my mother led the way, continuing to encourage us to attend church. By encouraging, I mean sometimes she had to drag us out of bed, and at times, she had to resort to strong-arm tactics. Nonetheless, being exposed to the constant word of God and the light of Christ, allowed my soul to begin to heal. Not all of my *joy* began to be restored, but bits and pieces that I had surrendered to God began to heal inside of my heart, even though my circumstances were often painful at school. Still, a wave of silent anger brewed deeply in my heart. Clearly, I had more forgiving and surrendering to do.

My mother was keeping a secret in her heart too: we basically had no money. It weighed on her tremendously. As a single mom, trying to keep up and ahead of the piling bills seemed almost impossible. She was in constant struggle in her heart, torn between wanting to stay at home to raise us girls or put food on the table. The power in our home would constantly be turned off. I remember at times watching television and lifting my feet as I saw mice running through the living room because the house was old and we couldn't afford an exterminator. When the plumbing went out in the kitchen and she couldn't afford to fix it, we simply did the dishes in the bathtub. When the laundry machine didn't work she hung our clothes on the back clothesline to dry.

In desperation, my mother took small jobs at the local canary. She would drop us off at school in the morning, sew for private clients, work at the fabric store, pick us up from school, and then after dinner, stand in the assembly line sorting beans on the conveyor belt. She worked so hard and still wasn't able to stay ahead. At one point, she picked strawberries and beans in the fields to earn extra money and bring home fresh fruit that was too expensive for us to afford in the grocery store.

I remember the *joy* on our faces and in our hearts when the local farmer would kindly drop off the extra milk from his farm—it was the best milk I had ever tasted in my life. My mouth almost had a heart attack the first time I tasted this farm-fresh cold milk, as milk in *my* home consisted of powdered carnation milk-mix that I would put in my water, stir, and pretend it was milk. We couldn't afford a hot lunch at school, but I'm so thankful for those meals looking back as sometimes food in our home was scarce and that school meal was something balanced and nutritious that I always looked forward to eating.

One thing that wasn't scarce or in short supply in our home was love. There was always plenty of hugs and love to go around, which was a blanket of comfort to my soul. My mother continued to be summoned to the principal's office to discuss my out-of-control behavior. When boys hit me, called me names, or touched me, I would chase them around the schoolyard ready to viciously attack back. The extent of my retaliation intensified with my unchecked anger. I remember one incident that began during fifth-grade math. While I was at the drinking fountain in the back of class a boy was behind me waiting for some water. After I finished drinking, he asked me a question. I looked at him perplexed, and he proceeded to reach out and inappropriately grab me. I was enraged. That moment, all the rage inside me surfaced, and I lunged at him with a voracity that I didn't know was inside me. In my mindless rage, I grabbed a small piece of his hair, and ripped it out of his head as he began to run—fast! All of this drama took place inside the classroom as I chased after him screaming, "I'll get you for this," as he dodged in and out of desks. My behavior was so irrational that I hadn't yet figured out what I was going to do with the boy once I caught him. All that my ten-year-old instincts impressed upon me was that I was going to leave a mark on this boy somehow. My feverish, unrelenting chase was punctuated by the poor homeroom teacher yelling "STOP" several times. I was in big trouble yet again and was marched to the principal's office for the umpteenth time.

Despite what seems like a no-win situation, the picture I'm describing actually had glimpses of hope. Despite my deeply-seated anger, I had a new sense of *JOY* because God constantly reminded me of His love for me. It was that new strength and courage that determined me to stand up for myself—to not be a victim. God was on my side and if God would be for me, then who could be against me, right? My logic was confused, though, because fighting and standing up for myself ultimately took its toll on me and my heart.

I hadn't realized at that tender age that God keeps His promises in His word. It was my emotions that were jumping ahead of me in the learning process. It would take a greater understanding of God's teachings before I could bring my emotions under control and allow full *joy* back into my life. I committed to allowing more of God into my life—into those painful areas that I had kept closed off, shut down, and hidden. HE would bring me *joy* as I trusted in HIM.

> The Lord will fight [your battles] for you, you need only be still.
> (Exodus 14:14 NIV)

What became exceedingly clear was that I had to address the big secret I was hiding from the world or it would continue to eat up my soul. At the time I didn't have the ability to comprehend its full impact on my life, but I knew that I had to tell someone about it. The big secret was that when I was 7 years old, I was raped by our long-time family friend's son. It held a powerful grip over me as I seethed with unforgiveness and anger.

Thoughts would team through my head as I looked in the mirror. *You are not enough . . . you are bad . . . no one could love you . . . you are dirty . . . you are worthless . . . you are used . . . you are nothing . . . you are ugly . . .* on and on it went. Not able to shut off my mind, these powerful words and lies of the enemy deceived my mind because of the constant shame I carried twenty-four hours a day, seven days a week. Binge eating became my destructive therapy, and I would eat way more than my stomach could hold. I was unwittingly hurting myself because I still believed I was bad, unworthy, and worthless. Eating and hurting myself dulled out the pain of the feelings and voices that constantly swam around in my head.

When you are done hurting, you can move into healing.
(Brenda Epperson-Moore)

One night while I was in middle school, my mom ran down the street to my aunt's house for a couple of minutes. My sister was out with friends, and I was alone in the house with our big German Shepherd dog, Sparky, in case anything went wrong. The other thing my mom left me with was a tray full of freshly-baked brownies. As I was watching television with Sparky, the smell of the hot-out-of-the-oven brownies permeated my every fiber. The sweet aroma wafted around, circling my head. Teasingly, they were calling my name. I recall the turmoil inside my head vividly. I was lonely, friend-less, an outcast, fat, and the principal's worst nightmare. I imagined that if I scarfed down a few brownies, I would feel *joy* again. Mom always cooked enough food for a football team—even though there were only three of us! As I approached the jumbo-sized warm brownie tray with chocolate still dripping down the side of the warm baking dish, I began to eat and eat and eat and eat until they were all gone. My actions remind me of that book, *The Very Hungry Caterpillar*. I'm pretty sure I looked like him too by the time I was done. The *joy* of the taste lasted only for a minute or two. What followed was torturous pain.

As I lay on the couch in absolute misery and out of control, another kind of pain crept up on the scene: the physical pain of my stomach crying out for mercy after the abuse I had meted out to it. I don't recall anything after that because I passed out like a light. The only recollection I have is of being woken up by my mom screaming with terror, Sparky my German shepherd barking frantically, and my aunt on top of me yelling, "Wake up, Brenda, wake up! Please God, wake up!" Finally, opening my eyes, seeing my mother crying, and coming into consciousness, I thought what in the world had happened? I had eaten myself into a food coma. My world spi-raled, and I was going down fast. That's what happens when we try to find temporary *joy* in the world in any substance or drug. Sooner or later the pain comes right back.

God promises to be your exceeding or abundant *joy*.

Fearing for my health, my mother wisely took me in to see a doc-tor. After several tests, I was diagnosed as a border-line diabetic. I was convinced it was because the brownies were still in my system, but I knew enough to realize that I had to lose weight and radically change my food intake, or I was headed down the insulin road. I needed strength from God, and I needed it that day—not the next day! My sense of power was weak and unwilling, I realized I was *powerless*. So, I turned to *The One* who had never let me down. In my darkest hour, He was always there to give me strength and encouragement. I would learn that my true power came not when I was standing up and fighting, but when I was kneeling down and praying. I began to look at the book of Psalms, which says, "Look to the Lord and His strength; seek *His* face always" (Psalm 105:4 NIV).

> You have loved righteousness and hated wickedness; Therefore God, your God has set you above your companions by anointing you with the oil of *joy*. (Hebrews 1:9 NIV)

> But the fruit of the spirit is love, *joy*, peace, patience, kindness, goodness, faithfulness, gentleness and self-control. Against such things there is no law. (Galatians 5:22 NIV)

One of the reasons Jesus was anointed with *joy* far above anyone else is because He loved righteousness and hated wickedness. The fruit listed in Galatians 5 is Jesus' character, as well as his nature. When we become Christians, or believers, or followers of Christ, our spirits are identical to Christ Jesus. We all have these gifts inside of us if we would just dare to believe in ourselves, through God's love, and use them.

> The pain you've been feeling, can't compare to the joy that's coming. (Romans 8:18 paraphrase)

Recently I attended a funeral for a young boy who died suddenly and unexpectedly in his bed. He went to bed in the evening one night and didn't wake up. He hadn't even completed his seventh-grade year. We were all terribly heartbroken. While at the memorial to honor his life, I was completely stunned as his brave mother, who stood before everyone grieving, began to share some of her son's short life and the impact he had made, not only in her life but also in others. The mother's strength had an immediate effect: one by one, coaches, teachers, friends, and family stood up to share how this young boy impacted their life. Do you know what was so amazing? Each one of them talked about how much *joy* this boy had brought to their hearts and lives. Each one of them talked about the fact that no matter what he was facing, he was filled with this infectious *joy*. The *joy* that this precious boy carried caused others to draw to him, to lean on him in his young life, and to desire what he had, because it made them feel so good. That boy's *joy* lifted others from children to adults. Whether he knew it or not, that *joy* was from God. You see, *joy* has no age limits. *Joy* isn't something we should stop pursuing because we are older. Have you ever heard anyone saying, "Why are you so excitedly happy? You're acting like a child," or, "You have to grow up and not be so excited!" Who made up that rule?

Michael D. Lemonick wrote an article in *Time* about "The Biology of *Joy.*" Here's a quote by Lemonick:

> People who rate in the upper reaches of happiness on psychological tests develop about 50% more antibodies than average in response to flu vaccines, and that, says Davidson, "is a very large difference." Others have discovered that happiness or related mental states like hopefulness, optimism, and contentment appear to reduce the risk or limit the severity of cardiovascular disease, pulmonary disease, diabetes, hypertension, colds, and upper-respiratory infections as well. According to a Dutch study of elderly patients published in November, those upbeat mental states reduced an individual's risk of death 50% over the study's nine-year duration. Says Laura Kubzansky, a health psychologist at Harvard's School of Public Health, in a masterpiece of understatement: "There's clearly some kind of effect."[1]

Harvard also did one of the longest-running studies on *joy*. The *Harvard Gazette* article is entitled "Good genes are nice, but *joy* is better."[2] In this Harvard study on octogenarians, there is irrefutable evidence that embracing relationships within our communities helps us live longer, happier, and healthier lives.

Liz Mineo, Harvard Staff Writer, highlights these interesting findings: "Close relationships, more than money or fame, are what keep people happy throughout their lives, the study revealed. Those ties protect people from life's discontents, help to delay mental and physical decline, and are better predictors of long and happy lives than social class, IQ, or even genes."[3]

Robert Waldinger, the director of a seventy-five-year-old study on adult development, has unprecedented access to data on true happiness and satisfaction. In his TED talk, he shared three important lessons learned from

1. Lemonick, "Biology of Joy."
2. Mineo, "Good Genes."
3. Mineo, "Good Genes."

the study as well as some practical wisdom on how to build a fulfilling, long life:[4]

1. Marital satisfaction has a protective effect on people's mental health.

2. Those who maintained warm relationships with family and friends lived longer and happier lives, and the loners often died earlier.

3. Good relationships don't just protect our bodies; they protect our brains.

> Loneliness kills. It's as powerful as smoking or alcoholism. (Robert Waldinger)[5]

According to the *Huffington Post*:

> The simple act of a hug isn't just felt on our arms. When we embrace someone, oxytocin (also known as "the cuddle hormone") is released, making us feel all warm and fuzzy inside. The chemical has also been linked to social bonding. "Oxytocin is a neuropeptide, which basically promotes feelings of devotion, trust and bonding," DePauw University psychologist Matt Hertenstein told NPR. "It really lays the biological foundation and structure for connecting to other people."[6]

The biological foundation and structure for connecting to other people is evident in:

- More hugs = lower blood pressure.
- A hug may help alleviate our fears.
- Hugging can be good for our hearts.
- Adults benefit from hugging the most.[7]

According to researchers at Ohio State University, hugging, and physical touch becomes increasingly important with age. "The older you are, the more fragile you are physically, so contact becomes increasingly important for good health," University psychologist Janice Kiecolt-Glaser told *USA Today*.[8]

4. Mineo, "Good Genes."
5. Mineo, "Good Genes."
6. Holmes, "7 Reasons,."
7. Holmes, "7 Reasons."
8. Elias, "Hugs Warm."

Studies have shown that loneliness, particularly with age, can also increase stress and have adverse health effects. By hugging someone, we instantly feel closer to that person and decrease feelings of loneliness.[9]

Well-Hugged Babies Are Less Stressed as Adults

Want to do something for future generations? Hug them when they're still little. An Emory University study found a link between touch and relieving stress, particularly in the early stages of life. The research concluded that the same can be said of humans, citing that babies' development—including how they cope with stress as adults—depends on a combination of nature and nurture.[10]

In a study on fears and self-esteem, research published in the journal *Psychological Science* revealed that hugs and touch significantly reduce worry of mortality. The studies found that hugging—even if it was just an inanimate object like a teddy bear—helps soothe individuals' existential fears.[11]

> I want to affect the world and not let the world infect me!
> (Brenda Epperson-Moore)

So, let's all get out there and hug our family, friends, co-workers, animals, and even stuffed animals, and maybe an enemy or two. Just watch yourself, your world, your heart, and your mind change, soften and expand, as well as everyone and everything around you. Remember a hug is free, just like a smile or a kind word. So what's your excuse?

Let me ask you something. When's the last time you had a good hug? When's the last time you gave a hug to someone else? My life began to change demonstratively when I stopped looking at what I didn't have and really began to be thankful for what I did have. Gratitude multiplies how we see our situation, widens the lens of our lives, and gives us a new perspective.

Joel Osteen told a story about twin babies in ICU. One baby was much smaller and more sickly than the other. The smaller baby began to decline in health rapidly, so the doctors decided to put both babies—the stronger one and the weaker one—together in the same incubator. The next morning, much to the medical staff's surprise, the larger twin wiggled over to her sister and wrapped her arm around her weaker little sibling. What the staff

9. Holmes, "7 Reasons."

10. Hinman, "Well-hugged Babies."

11. Koole, "Touch."

noticed is how the sick twin became much stronger within a short period of time. Her pulse increased and her numbers began to elevate, all from the physical contact and comfort that her twin was providing.[12]

The same thing happened to my middle daughter. When she was born, her lungs were a little underdeveloped and she had to be put in an oxygen tent immediately after she was born. She was turning blue from the lack of oxygen, and my husband and I were both worried. What happened after that was significant. While I was recovering in the hospital from a c-section, not able to go to my daughter, my husband instinctively left me and went right into the room where our daughter lay alone in an oxygen crib, and that's where the nurses witnessed something incredible. The moment my husband started touching and caressing our daughter, she started breathing normally, and her numbers began to level out as more oxygen ran through her body. Her body responded appreciatively with life-affirming color returning to her cheeks and the rest of her little body. Imagine that. All it took was a loving touch for our baby girl to build her strength and heal. Please try it. I know that it works!

Prayer

Even when we feel lonely, we know according to your word that you promise to never leave us or forsake us. Lord Jesus, comfort anyone reading this book who may feel alone, abandoned, or rejected. Restore them, strengthen them, and fill them with your overwhelming love. Give them a supernatural hug filled with your love. No more self-pity, no more self-doubt. Fill us with a breakthrough, breaking forward motivation that changes the environment for supernatural miracles to occur. How? We invite you Jesus into our situation, and when you show up, miracles occur. So we welcome you into these anxious feelings and wait expectantly for relief and miracles. You are not forgotten. You are not alone. In Jesus' name.

12. Osteen, "Become a Miracle."

Challenge Questions

1. Have you given someone a hug today? If not, or if you can't, hug yourself as a reminder of how very special you are. Write three things you love about yourself

2. Do you only do things for others that you know can pay you back? If so, how can you change that mindset?

3. What is one selfless act that you can do for a stranger today?

4. If you had no fear, how would you live your life differently?

5. Have you read your Bible today? If not, open it now and allow God to speak to your heart. Write the verse down that he shows you and memorize it.

4

Be Bold, Don't Lose Hope

BEING BOLD CAN BE a character trait, or it can start with a conscious thought of strong positive emotions that overwhelm us into being bolder. After the passing out on the couch incident and tons of blood work later, my family learned that I had the onset of diabetes. The doctors indicated that I may or may not grow out of it, but I would certainly need to be monitored. That diagnosis scared me as I knew much of my pain was self-induced because when I hurt myself physically, the pain in my heart, mind, and soul would quiet down.

Still, my mother was adamant about us attending church, as well as being involved in every program, concert, ribbon-cutting ceremony, or event that the church was sponsoring. I really enjoyed going to the youth groups at church on Wednesday evenings as everyone there seemed to accept me, and they filled my heart with laughter and much-needed relief from the school week. Besides that, the meetings were fun and interesting.

Junior high for me felt like torture, girls were talking about boys and having sex, I was size 14—heavier than ever—and no real friendships seemed to emerge for me. Kids did a lot of experimenting with drugs, and some suicides began to occur, which overwhelmed my heart with pain. Even now lately, there has been what seems like an incredible amount of suicides on the rise. Not just of those who are what some may consider, down on their luck, but those who are considered successful. For instance, the shocking suicides of Kate Spade and Anthony Bourdain. They were successful people who seemed to have everything to live for, yet still took their own lives. My husband recently attended the funeral of a young boy not quite finished from high school who also took his own life. Not only those in the spotlight are committing suicide but what about all of the countless other nameless, faceless souls whose lives have been cut short due to suicide? We may not know their names, but God does, and I know His heart grieves over this tragedy sweeping rampant across our country.

According to a new government study, suicide has been on the rise since 1999.[1] Why? Is it mental illness, loneliness, depression, anxiety, over-medicating ourselves, or not using medication when it's needed for temporary support? Is it the fact that more churches are closing, and fewer people feel the need to be a part of a community of believers or be a part of anything? Is it because we connect more to our phones and computers rather than with people? Or maybe it's because we settle. We settle for what we see with our eyes rather than what we believe. We settle for mediocrity. We settle when we value the wrong things and expect those things to make us happy. We settle and believe the lies of unkind, malicious words spoken over us. We settle for lies rather than daring to believe the truth. We settle when we refuse to forgive and release that person or situation and instead carry a big heavy ugly trash bag around with us all of our lives. I'm calling us all to *Rise Up* out of death into forgiveness and a beautiful fresh fullness of life that God wants for all of us.

New York Magazine published a story about the "New York face." It stated that people are much more overwhelmed, depressed, anxious, and stressed than ever before. They actually drew happy faces on people's faces instead of the sad looks people were walking around within the random pictures that were taken. The article by Adam Sternbergh interviewed Professor Laurie Santos who stated, "College students are much more overwhelmed, much more stressed, much more anxious, and much more depressed than they've ever been." Then Santos went on to say, "I don't think it's just in colleges." "According to a recent survey by the American College Health Association, 52 percent of students reported feeling hopeless, while 39 percent suffered from such severe depression they found it difficult to function at times."[2] Did you know that America ranked eighteenth in the U.N.'s "World Happiness Report?"[3]

In severely depressed patients (as well as mildly depressed), some doctors have asked their patients to make a gratitude journal and every day write down three things they are grateful for. As was quoted earlier in the

---

1. https://www.cdc.gov/vitalsigns/suicide/index.html.
2. Sternbergh, "How to Be Happy."
3. Sternbergh, "How to Be Happy."

book, "Write things down and make it plain on a tablet." This helps our brain connect to the reality of what we are moving toward and connects us to the reality of what we cannot yet see. Add a cup of faith for an explosive unstoppable destiny.

> A lot of people think of happiness as a very, very exciting emotion. They expect it to be this constant state of ecstasy-as opposed to equanimity, which is a more sustainable and attainable form of happiness, almost like a quiet joy. It doesn't look like winning the lottery. It looks much more like sitting quietly and noticing that your life is actually wonderful. (Hedy Kober)[4]

Remember earlier I said it's not just material things or situations that should ultimately bring us *joy*? What I'd like you to do is stop, sit down, and take an inventory of the things that make you happy and bring you *joy*. What are they? Who are they? How many times a day do you count your money or check your bank account, Facebook, Instagram, or financial status? We count our money, we count our social media followers, right? Now let's start counting our blessings, name them one by one, and it will open your eyes to see what God has done.

Write down three things today, right now, that you are grateful for? Make them as small or as complex as you'd like.

1.

2.

3.

According to Dr. Don Colbert

> 10 minutes of belly laughter is like internal aerobics. The diaphragm, thorax, abdomen, heart, lungs, and even the liver are given a massage during a hearty laugh.[5]

What an amazing gift God has given us. Dr. Colbert goes on to say,

> When we laugh, powerful chemicals called endorphins, which act much the same way as morphine, are released in the brain. Endorphins trigger a feeling of well-being throughout your entire body, which can burn 1.3 calories per minute.[6]

4. Sternbergh, "How to Be Happy," quote from Guest Lecture "Keep It Down."
5. Colbert, *Deadly Emotions*, 186.
6. Colbert, *Deadly Emotions*, 186.

So, you see laughter is like medicine!

Here's what he goes on to say about laughter,

> Its powerful effects on the human body are unprecedented, and always available if we just allow ourselves to feel real, deep, *joy*. Approximately 10 minutes of laughter causes a hormone to be released that relaxes you and even allows you to sleep easier. This same laughter releases a hormone that can help relieve depression. For such a simple act, laughter could almost be described as the miracle cure![7]

Dr. Colbert actually prescribes ten belly laughs a day for some of his patients.

#I*JOY I AM JESUS ON YOU*

Joy is free. *Joy* is a gift. It's our birthright. We need to not only open and accept this gift, but we must be also willing to put it on and share that gift of *joy* with others #I*JOY*. What I'm suggesting is you choose *joy*, put it on like a beautiful perfume or your finest outfit, and then give *joy* away to others.

When I was in middle school times were tough as a young teenager. I didn't fit in. We couldn't afford the right designer clothes or shoes, and I was still carrying around so much extra weight, from the shame of the rape, and all of the bad eating habits I developed. Once I started in middle school, every summer I wrote in a journal. I wrote what I was thankful for and began to set small personal goals for myself in what I liked to call my "dream goals." These were things that I could possibly attain if I prayed, invited God into my situation to give me strength, worked hard, implemented strategies to reach my goal, and stay focused. I also incorporated things that I could do to help others, so it was not just a list about myself. For example, my list would include: changing my eating habits, more exercise, gratitude journal, rescue stray animals, taking up tennis, walking my dogs regularly, riding my bike in the park with friends, singing at a retirement home, volunteering to help clean up our local park, painting our church, and volunteering at the church summer camp. Every year, with a lot of hard work, I would lose approximately ten to fifteen pounds, keep it off, and return to school a little smaller, a little more confident, and able to share with my friends about all the people I helped, which then inspired my them to become more proactive. I learned early on in life that setting goals big and small helped me focus and actually strategically accomplish those things I had been putting off. I believe it's so important to set what I call 'wild goals.' These are things

7. Colbert, *Deadly Emotions*, 187.

that are so far out of reach they literally scare you. It's been said that if your goals or dreams don't scare you they're not big enough.

"We are only as blind as we want to be." (Maya Angelou)

Every year our church would gather the middle school and high school students and bring us to this beautiful camp in the mountains of Central Oregon. It was filled with two weeks of fun. Hiking, swimming, sports camping, and spending time with friends away from school. So when the opportunity came to volunteer at the church summer camp in this beautiful mountain resort in Central Oregon, I jumped at the chance. I signed up as a kitchen volunteer, which then helped pay for my summer camp as we couldn't afford the tuition. Much to my surprise, they ended up moving me from kitchen help to part-time camp counselor. I enjoyed being with the kids, playing games with them, taking long walks and hikes as well as attending church services with the children in the evening.

I remember while on the camping trip feeling bad about this one young girl who wore braces on her legs and spent much of the time watching the other kids run and play sports. I would sit with her and we would find other things to do together, but I could tell her heart longed to run and play with the others.

Spending so much time with the kids allowed me to really get to know them on an individual basis. They began to open up and trust me, one by one I began to hear about their stories. The kids would talk about deep hurts, insecurities, challenges in life at home, school difficulties, trials, and triumphs.

The week was coming to an end and sadly camp was almost over. I poured as much of myself into these kids as I could as a young girl myself still trying to figure life out. I found it so rewarding hearing their hearts and hopefully being able to help them with unanswered questions, or at times, just being a listening ear. That final evening there was a special speaker during the evening service whom I will never forget. His name was Alton Garrison. As he spoke you could feel the electric high voltage power of God at work. He passionately spoke to us about God's love and the power of the Holy Spirit, reminding us and challenging us to believe that God still heals. I could hardly keep up with my notes as every word he spoke seemed to be a nugget of truth about life and healing that penetrated my soul. Then, as the music began to play he had an altar call and asked kids if they would like to come forward for prayer or healing or to ask Jesus into their hearts.

Some of the kids sprung up and began to almost run to the altar. These kids were anywhere from the ages of seven to ten, I was all of fourteen myself.

As I saw the altar begin to fill up with kids I was nudged by the Holy Spirit to join the children and pray for them and over them. I walked up to the front of the altar to pray for some of these children who were weeping uncontrollably under the power and presence of the almighty living God. I gave all I had in prayer for these lives to be transformed and know the power of God. Keep in mind this was a small little log cabin they used for church services during summer camp in the middle of the beautiful green mountains of central Oregon. No cameras, no sensationalism. Just a piano, trees, fresh mountain air, and the power of God. That evening the power of God's presence was so tangible, you could feel something was happening. To me, it was a familiar love, similar to the same love I felt wrapped around me all those years ago as a young girl when I gave my life to Christ, which then began to overwhelm my heart, mind, and soul. The power of the Holy Spirit was so present lives were being healed before my eyes. Nobody was prepared for what we saw next. I was so engulfed in praying for this one girl, who was sobbing, when all of a sudden the speaker Alton Garrison said, "Look, everyone." We all looked up tears streaming down our faces and, there she was, that same young girl who was sent to camp with the leg braces standing on the small platform, crying and shaking. The power of God all over her. Then suddenly, in front of us all, Alton said, "Take off those braces and walk, you are healed in Jesus' name." That's exactly what she did. She took off her braces and walked across the platform completely healed. Even recalling this moment gives me goosebumps. The log cabin was silent, then we erupted in loud thunderous clapping and an outcry to God like I have never heard of before. I had never seen or experienced anything like the power of God that hit that little chapel. Kids were filled with the power of the Holy Spirit, healing erupted, and children began speaking in tongues and rejoicing over this young girl's life being transformed and healed right before our eyes. Another young girl took all of her pills and flushed them down the toilet as all of her pain in her body was gone. This was supernatural and could have only come from the hand of God. To this day I have no idea how long we were in that small log cabin in the woods, but from that moment on, no one could ever tell me there wasn't a God. A *big* God who still heals today!

> Lord my God, I called to you for help, and you healed me.
> (Psalm 30:2 NIV)

The next day we all went home; changed, saved, healed, ignited, and excited for all God was going to do in all of our lives. Upon telling my mom and dad what happened on those mountains of Oregon, they were stunned. The one thing my parents said to me over and over again was, "God showed you all of this so you could go tell others and change the world." I have held those words close in my heart to this day.

My mother's new and forever marriage to my father was a beautiful one. It was a match made in heaven, literally. My father reached out to my mom across the oceans via mail, before email existed, and they began a love affair through correspondence. He has been a steady in my life and an incredible partner for my mother. They were married for over thirty years. Sadly, my dear father recently died. Their love and marriage was a profound example in my life, and I am so thankful for that.

High school had its challenges, but there was a growing burning flame inside my heart and soul that I was meant for more. Through my achievements of small goal setting through the summers and the camp revival experience, it made me realize that there are infinite possibilities out there just waiting for me to grab. Upon entering my sophomore year of high school, I began to try out for things I would never have tried before. I auditioned for the jazz vocal group and was accepted. I tried out for the tennis team and found myself on the varsity team as a freshman. I even dared to try out for Miss Oregon Teen USA. After a few tries and much persistence, I won and was crowned Miss Oregon United Teenager, a title my older sister had previously won! Then I petitioned for my school student council, which required me to speak in front of the entire High school! Well wouldn't you know, my sister Deborah campaigned for me, made my posters, and probably threatened her friends to vote for me or else, and after a lot of hard work it, yep, you guessed it, I was elected chairperson over the entire high school! Leadership seemed to really suite me, working side by side with the fabulous female vice principal brought a new excitement into my life. I went from this teased, overweight, angry, hating myself, outcast, argumentative girl to a young woman who was a leader and began to achieve, reaching for goals and actually accomplishing them.

Leadership gave me a new perspective on life. Those around me began to respect me and ask me for advice. I had to do the work inside my heart and in my own life for it to reflect outside of my life. These accomplishments gave me *joy* and a sense of purpose that my life was making a difference and the things that seemed impossible were suddenly possible. I quickly realized my dreams were not even big enough, that I needed to dream bigger, reach further toward God, and reach further toward the world and others in my heart. No matter what age you are or how much money you have or don't have, your life matters. You have a purpose here on earth, and you can reach people and relate to people no one else can simply because of who you are. Don't let your dreams fade away. Don't believe the lie that you just exist and nothing you do will make a difference. Don't get into agreement with that false narrative over your life. You are so significant and important to God. He knows you by name. You are critically important to your community and to the world, but I really believe it starts small then moves into something big. You are only one decision away from changing the course of your future. Every good thing you do and every prayer you pray makes a difference. Every step you take toward forgiveness, every life you touch and help, every dream you dream, brings you one step closer to changing your life, your home, your community, and the world, so get to dreaming. Go, do, live, be, and don't forget to HOPE. Hold On, Pain Ends. Take the healing power of the cross, be healed, and then, hand that healing to others. Anything is possible if you believe.

Prayer

As we keep our eyes fixed on you God, release us from fear and depression, expand our borders and territory beyond what we see, and keep us excited, *joy*ful, and expectant for our future. Show us the wisdom of good daily decisions. I command in Jesus name that you dispatch warring angels to heal us and remind us who we are in you, oh Lord. Give us strategies, dreams, and visions that are in alignment with your word and your will and purpose for our lives. Thy will be done on earth as it is in heaven.

Challenge Questions

1. What is one dream or goal you have dreamed about but never accomplished? Write one small step you can take toward this goal.

2. Name one or two wild goals you'd like to see happen in your life or in the world?

3. What's one step you could take to move closer to wise decisions for today? This can be as simple as staying away from unhealthy foods, people, or conversations. Write it down and do it.

4. What is something that is causing imbalance in your life? This may also be medications, unhealthy thinking or habits, or relationships that are causing you to become stagnant.

5. What can you do to make a difference in someone else's life? Remember it can even be something small: opening a door for a stranger or complimenting someone on their outfit or their beautiful smile.

6. Challenge yourself to do something you never thought you could do? Write it down and do it today. This can be as simple as staying away from sugar for a day or a week or not having one complaint come out of your mouth for an hour, a few days or a lifetime. Make this challenge as simple or as hard as you can. This will expand and ultimately change your life.

5

When Did Life Become So Serious?

A merry heart does good like a medicine:
but a broken spirit dries the bones.

—PROVERBS 17:22 NIV

WHEN DID WE BECOME so serious in life? I remember being in a restaurant and this becoming a poignant question as I laughed out loud, not obnoxiously, but just a good belly laugh, and people turned to either give me a dirty look or make a derogatory comment. People have actually yelled across a restaurant, "be quiet." It is mind baffling that this type of response comes from such an innocent act of *joy*.

> Surely He will save you from the fowler's snare and from the deadly pestilence. (Psalm 91:3 NIV)

I've seen it with my own eyes. So many of us are walking around like the fowler mentioned in Psalm 91. We are just waiting to trap each other with words we did or didn't say, or we are, ourselves, caught in a trap. Read this definition below of the fowler.

FOWLER
foul'-er (yoqesh):
A professional bird-catcher. In the days previous to firearms, birds were captured with nets spread on the ground, in traps and snares.[1]

---

1. Bible Study Tools, "Fowler."

There was a method of taking young birds from a nest and raising them by hand, and when they had become very tame, they were confined in hidden cages so that their voices would call others of their kind to the spot, and they could be killed by arrows of concealed bowmen or by the use of the throw-stick. This was a stick 1 1/2 feet in length and 1/2 inch in diameter, hurled with a rotary motion at the legs of the birds. It was very effective when thrown into flocks of ground birds, such as partridge or quail, especially if the birds were running uphill.

There was also a practice of sewing a captured bird's eyelids together and confining it so that its horrific cries for help would call large numbers of birds through curiosity, and when those birds arrived, they too could then be taken, caught, and trapped. These fowlers knew the art of deception, and so does Satan. Like these birds when our eyes are sewn shut by our own sin, we become trapped and ensnared.

Perhaps you are already in a trap, and you cannot get out. Your eyes have been sewn shut as the definition talks about, and you can't even see anymore. Or maybe you are caught in the trap or cage of anger, bitterness, illness, brokenness, resentment, unforgiveness, anxiety, loneliness, and *joy-lessness*. I was so stunned when I read the definition of "fowler" and how birds were caught, blinded, and then used as bait to ensnare other birds. It hit me so strongly that many of us are in cages, trapped in, believing, or even living a lie. We become so miserable that we then ensnare others into believing that lie: ourselves, our co-workers, children, parents, family, friends. I have seen and prayed with so many people who live in fear, afraid of the truth, afraid of who they are, afraid to live in freedom because they have been ensnared, trapped, and their eyes have been sewn shut with fear and lies.

Here is a promise that God made to David and all of us. The Almighty will deliver us from the evil plans set before us that rob and steal our *joy*, peace, and happiness.

> Our soul escaped as a bird of the snare of the fowlers.
> (Psalm 124:7 KJV)

There is a powerful story of redemption, a true story of a man named John Newton, born approximately 1725 AD. He was a slave trader who worked on the slave ships bringing people back and forth to and from distant lands who were caught and bound to be bought and sold. He later went from working on the ship to becoming the captain of this wretched slave vessel. John Newton's eyes were sewn shut, he had forgotten about humanity; he believed the lie that slavery was right. As the story goes, one day the ship was caught in a terrible storm at sea which ripped a hole in the bottom of the vessel. Having heard about Christianity, but never giving it much thought, in that moment of desperation John Newton cried out to God and begged for his life and also the lives on the ship, and he made a deal with God that if God would rescue him and his ship, he would give his life over to God. The ship limped into the harbor safely, and John Newton remembered his promise to God. Through the powerful love of God, John Newton's eyes were opened. John's willingness to surrender to God caused him to see others in a totally different way. He went from being a carrier of human bondage to a champion of freedom, and he fervently worked much of his life to abolish slavery. John Newton went on to become a priest, and he collaborated and wrote some of our greatest hymns we still sing to this day, one of which is Amazing Grace—how sweet the sound indeed.

> I am not what I ought to be, I am not what I want to be, I am not what I hope to be in another world, but still, I am not what I once used to be, and by the grace of God I am what I am. (John Newton)

Just like God's promises, He will help us escape the trappings of this world, open our eyes, set us free from the bondage of fear, anxiety, and depression, and fill us with "*joy* unspeakable." Don't let yourself be caught in the trap, day after day, night after night, where all you do is sit and cry, bound, trapped in pain from the past, feeling unloved, abandoned, or alone with a heart that cannot find rest. I believe when our eyes have been sewn shut because of either our own sin, others sin, bad decisions, the pain passed down to us when we were a child, or life's difficulties, we lose our grip on what is right; we lose gratitude and hope. But God's *joy* is absolute, and He promises to give us freedom and *joy* if we dare to accept it.

Are we afraid of *joy*? I think today some of us are actually afraid of *joy. Joy*, and finding *joy* is a radical act these days. I remember being in a grocery store one day, feeling so happy I wanted to burst. While walking to the checkout line, I walked past a woman, I smiled widely and said, "Hi, how are you?" She actually looked me straight in the eye, grabbed her purse tightly, and moved away like I was going to snatch her purse! I thought, what has happened to us that we are so afraid or so cynical that we cannot even respond when someone greets us. Have we forgotten *how* to respond and say hello back? What has robbed us of such *joy* that we cannot inter- act freely and with the best intentions with humanity? When did our eyes become sewn shut to the absolute freedom and *joy* that God wants us to walk and overflow in?

Did you know that when you smile at someone you are actually giving them a gift? *Yes!* A gift of *JOY*. It's *free,* and it's freeing. I have tried it several times and what I've discovered is that it's irrelevant whether I am feeling terrific wearing a fantastic outfit with my hair freshly blown out or if I am coming from the gym drenched in sweat and feeling sticky. Ninety percent of the time when I smile, the same response always happens. Yep, you guessed it! A smile comes back to me no matter what I look like.

Rise up in *JOY* (#IJOY), one of the fruits of the spirit that is so important in our lives, and yet, it's seemingly small and underestimated. That's why I felt so passionate about writing this book. Writing this book is an incredible act of obedience and faith for me. Never in a million years would I have imagined God opening this door for me.

Did you know that gratitude brings us *joy*? There is a saying that a happy heart is a healthy heart. Well, in the same way, gratitude allows us to stop focusing on ourselves and actually see others, so we can be a blessing. I don't know about you, but when all I do is think about myself or what I need and want or what I have or don't have, my heart begins to weigh down with cares or concerns that I was never meant to carry. When we reach outside of ourselves to see others who might not have it as good as we do, our eyes begin to open, and we begin to see that, perhaps, we have something to give to others that are in need. According to studies, when we fill a need for others, the feeling we receive is better than chocolate, or even sex!

Dr. Caroline Leaf has done extensive studies and research on our mental state and the brain. She explains in her books how our thoughts have a direct effect on our physical well-being. Joyce Meyer calls it "No more stinkin' thinkin.'" Here's what Dr. Leaf has to say about toxic thoughts:

> Up to 80 percent of physical, emotional, and mental health issues could be a direct result of our thought lives. The average person has over 30,000 thoughts a day. Through an uncontrolled thought life, we create the conditions for illness; we make ourselves sick! Research shows that fear, all on its own, triggers more than 1,400 known physical and chemical responses and activates more than 30 different hormones. There are intellectual and medical reasons to forgive! Toxic waste generated by toxic thoughts contributes to the following illnesses: diabetes, cancer, asthma, skin problems,

and allergies—to name just a few. Consciously control your thought life and start to detox your brain![2]

Medical research increasingly points to the fact that thinking and consciously controlling your thought life is one of the best ways, if not the best way, of detoxing your brain. It allows you to get rid of those toxic thoughts and emotions that can consume and control your mind.

Other factors that can affect our thought life. Did your mother ever say to you when you were younger, "You need to take a nap, you are crabby?" Did you know that good sleep patterns can extend your life? The necessary amount of sleep can also increase your physical performance athletically. There have been studies maintaining that while we sleep, harmful proteins and toxins that build up in our brain are actually washed away! So, sleeping is actually like a washing machine that cleans our brains, so we can be more clean, clear, and *joy*ful.

Have you ever noticed how when you clean your closet, your car, or your garage, and get rid of stuff that you don't need, you feel so much better? It's the same with our own lives. We are filled with so much junk that we can't en*joy* or find *joy* in our life or even see others with all the clutter around us.

Our family recently moved from the city to a smaller rural area and bought a small farm, as my kids are avid equestrians. It was like moving into two homes. We were setting up our human home and our animal home: the barn, the stalls, the tack rooms, *and* the home where our family lives. As I began the process of clearing out our previous home, it struck me how much junk we had saved over the years. I just never took the time to really take a look at the accumulation of stuff. All those little things add up to a lot of clutter. As I began to clear out drawer by drawer, room by room, I felt the nudge of God's hand saying, "Decluttering *does* matter. Look at all this clutter!" There was so much unnecessary stuff taking up room that there was little space for things that mattered and that we needed. I believe it's the same with our own lives and the emotional baggage and clutter we walk around with day after day. There's hardly room for anything else, let alone *joy*! When we put off clearing out the junk and clutter in our lives, I believe it blocks us from having a life filled with clarity, freedom, and a life that could be filled with more *joy*.

---

2. Leaf, *Who Switch Off My Brain*, 15.

I have a question for you, what if being thankful, speaking God scriptures daily or as much as possible was actually healing you, physically, mentally, and emotionally?

I am not a medical doctor. I am not a psychologist. I am not a therapist. I do not have a Ph.D. I am simply writing this book to share with you how God has radically, and completely, filled my own life with *joy*. It is an unimaginable quantity of *joy*, and it is full of glory!

Prayer

Open our eyes, oh God. Help us to not be bogged down with hate, apathy, criticism of others, and racism. Please release us into freedom so we will no longer be slaves to fear, anger, anxiety, bondage, and oppression. Release us from the clutter in our minds, emotions, hearts, and homes. Release us from the snares and entrapments of the world that would steal our time and rob us of our *joy* and energy, and refocus us to keep our eyes and ears open and completely fixed on you. We trust you, Lord, we believe that you will overturn every wrong and make us completely whole by the finished work on the cross. We decree and declare today a healing atmosphere around our lives. We reject depression and stand on the over three-thousand promises in the Bible for our lives. In Jesus' name.

Challenge Questions

1. What is one thing you could do today to clear out the clutter in your life? Maybe start with a drawer—open it and clean it.

2. How can you take a small step today to clear your mind, so you can make room for things that really matter and make room for more *joy*?

3. What is one thought you can identify today that is toxic and weighing you down?

4. Once identified, release this lie and ask God to replace it with His healing and *joy*.

5. Are you stuck in old ways or the world's way of doing things? Ask God to open your eyes to what is right, begin to change and release the stagnant destructive mindset. What is one thing the world says is okay that the Bible clearly states isn't right? Will you release this mindset and trust God to renew your thinking? Identify what it is, lay it down, and walk away from it.

6

Don't Confuse Small with Insignificant

COACH JOHN WOODEN WAS arguably the greatest basketball coach of all time, revered by Bill Walton, Kareem Abdul-Jabar, and other highly accomplished athletes. What's the one thing he taught his players first? Socks and shoelaces. Yes, the importance of small things. He believed that if you took the wrinkles out of your socks and insured that your shoelaces were firmly and properly tied, you would play a better game. It wasn't just a mental theory. He knew that the stopping, starting, and rapid directional turns that basketball athletes are required to do put exceptional pressure on their feet. Coach Wooden would say. "You tighten it up snugly by each eyelet. Then you tie it. And then you double-tie it so it won't come undone—because I don't want shoes coming untied during practice, or during the game."[1] His seemingly insignificant instruction on shoelaces was, in fact, very significant.

Have you ever noticed when you are at a sporting event how people appear to be so happy, excited, and engaged—that's only if their team is winning, of course. That is partially what makes sports venues such great places to visit. There is a vitally attractive, care-free spirit that permeates sporting events. People actually talk to strangers, happily sharing their opinions on players and strategy, unashamedly reaching out to people they'd typically ignore while walking down a street on a busy working day. Whether it's basketball, football, tennis, soccer, hockey, or baseball, there's a powerfully collective *joy* at every sports stadium that is fed by human connectedness and the soul-nourishing laughter that comes from that connection. I've always thought, "Lord, wouldn't this be great if we could carry this much *joy* around every day and carry that same *joy* into church, on the streets, in our

1. Gordon, "John Wooden."

homes and workplace?" The smiles, excitement, and free-flowing freedom ignite unity and acceptance that is so needed in the world today!

Athletes are such a special division of people. Their discipline, work ethic, and dedication require unimaginable commitment and sacrifice. They do the right things when nobody is watching them. Their mental strength sees them through the toughest times when there are injuries, loss, and disappointment. Skill can only take athletes halfway to their goal. Their physical stamina is dependent on their massive determination to work through the pain and exhaustion. The Olympic Games, to me, showcase the greatest human characteristics before our eyes. The Olympians make their standards of excellence look so easy and effortless, but there are thousands of hours of sweat and tears that go before the perfected fluidity of their movements. Every little piece of preparation towards their Olympic moment was done away from the cameras and everything mattered—even their shoelaces.

When I watched the movie, *The Greatest Showman*, this quote struck me, and I absolutely love the words:

The noblest art is that of making others happy. (P. T. Barnum)

I completely agree because when we purposely set out to be carriers of *joy*, which I call "*joy* carriers," we effect one of the greatest reactions from people. We give them *joy*, and in turn, our *joy* increases. I have seen it so often in my own life when I purposely look for something good or something nice to say to someone, even if that person is a stranger. The *joy* and happiness I see in their reaction help me to recognize that I can make a significant difference in the world every day. *Joy* is contagious, and through it, so many derivatives like gratitude become a part of the *joy* cycle.

I was in the grocery store and without making eye contact with me, the checkout lady seemed to be lost in her robotic world of dissatisfying scanning. I could barely hear her muffled words as she said with a sigh, "It's a busy day." One by one she scanned each food item, and then I saw her shoulders rise as she exhaled loudly and harder. Recognizing that she was having a really hard day, I said to her, "You know you are beautiful." She looked at me, froze, and said, "What?" I said it again. "You are so beautiful." She moved out of her trance, stopped what she was doing, finally looked at me, put her hand to her heart, and the most beautiful smile broke out on her face as she said, "Oh my gosh, thank you so much, you just made my day so much better." We began to engage in small talk and her face brightened, making her even more beautiful. The mundane task of scanning each item turned into laughter and fun. I was even having fun! You see, it's the small things, the little moments in life that affect everyone's *joy*. Just imagine if we all intentionally made that little bit of effort every day when going out into a cold, hard world; we'd create the opportunity to implant that little drop of *joy* and watch its unending ripple effect.

> Whenever you get a chance, put a drop of kindness into the pot of humanity. (Captain Wendell J. Furnas, POW in World War II)[2]

There are many scientifically-proven studies about breaking habits and negative behaviors. First, we must be aware that we have a behavior or a habit that is not benefitting us, or worse, holding us back. Imagine if, collectively, we started breaking the bad habit of never smiling? I encourage you to start today, along with me. You and I can break the bad habit of not being kind to others. By doing this, we remove the lie of it not mattering or not making a difference. It does matter, and it does make a difference! If every one of us created a new habit of smiling while looking directly into people's eyes, our impact could be as powerful as Mona Lisa's iconic smile. Do you know that Mona Lisa is one of the world's most important pieces of art? Your smile can become its own unique work of art—the art of making others happy. You *are* a work of art when the edges of your mouth move across your face, and your eyes twinkle. Your smile, laugh, and twinkle has inestimable healing properties for both you and the people who receive your gift.

According to V. S. Ramachandran, an Indian-American neuroscientist known for his experiments and theories in the human brain-behavior, "We're capable of mounting two different kinds of smiles: one genuine and the other forced. Each one, in fact, is generated in two separate parts of the brain. The smiles even look quite different which is why we can always tell one from the other with ease."[3]

To produce a genuine smile, we must feel like smiling. To smile at a stranger in a meaningful way requires that we muster some kind of empathetic feeling for them—that we care about someone we don't know, if only in a small way. For me, smiling at strangers is a small exercise of compassion. Studies have also shown that feelings often follow expressions. The

2. Furnas, "Obituaries."

3. Ramachandran, *Brief Tour*, 132.

expression of smiling (even if we don't feel like it) creates a positive change in our mood.

Some studies claim it takes twenty-one days to change a habit. Others say it takes longer depending on the link between the behavior and the habit. In other words, if you are trying to quit smoking, the chemical addiction combined with the physical act of picking up the cigarette, lighting it, and the satisfaction of smoking it, all make it a difficult habit to break. This may take months or years to break.

What I want us to look at are the circumstances around the habit because that's the trigger. Let's say you are trying to stop driving twenty-five miles above the speed limit, but if you are constantly leaving your house late, not giving yourself enough time, and rushing to make it to your destination, those actions will trigger that habit. If you can rearrange your schedule and discipline yourself enough to leave thirty minutes before your usual departure time, you will be more relaxed, and the trigger won't kick in. Regardless of whether you are trying to overcome an addiction that is physical, mental, or emotional, establishing a new pattern or reward will help and then heal that broken part of your life. That doesn't mean the urge won't ever be there, but when you establish a valuable reward from breaking a bad habit, the reward significantly redirects our habits towards better behavioral patterns.

> The secret of your future is hidden in your daily routine.
> (Max Lucado)

I believe so strongly in the power of prayer and the healing that comes from the word of God. There is life in the word of God, keys to our future that unlock the doors of our mind, body, soul, and spirit. I intentionally set my alarm and wake up early because I know the benefits of my daily routine of reading the Bible purposefully. Some days, God speaks to me in such powerful ways. Some days, I can barely get through one verse and have no idea what I just read. I also have a "Book of Promises" that I've sprinkled throughout this book of particularly meaningful verses to me that I read and confess out of my mouth almost every day over my life, my family, my home, my children, my dreams, and the future. I have actually seen some of these scriptures fulfilled, which has given me an uplifting amount of *joy* and victory over things that I thought would never come to pass. Will you join me and make these small changes in your life that will have a huge impact and outcome on the rest of the world?

Prayer

You are a God who sees. You are a God who makes the impossible possible. Help us to have big faith in the midst of unknowing and uncertainty. Remind us and reassure us that the only limits we put on ourselves are the limits we put on you. We lay down unhealthy mindsets and cancel dysfunctional words spoken over our lives. Increase our faith as we seek you with all of our hearts and remind us that big growth starts with the small seed, idea, or deed. Release your unlimited potential over your people today! Amen.

Challenge Questions

1. What's one thing you could add to your daily routine that would bring you and others more *joy*?

2. What's one thing you need to walk away from that is stealing your *joy*?

3. Start today by reading the book of Psalm or wherever God is leading you. Ask God to give you a revelation of what He wants to reveal to you in His word.

4. You can defeat big obstacles with one small stone like David did (1 Samuel 17). Our words can create obstacles in our lives, change your words, change your life. What words or thoughts can you change or add to your vocabulary that will radically change your life and future?

7

Keep Dreaming

DID YOU KNOW YOU can see your vision more clearly by approximately ninety percent if you simply write your dreams down? Writing down what you desire is powerful. It's even more powerful if you strategically write your goals with measurable milestones along the way. According to a study done by Gail Matthews at Dominican University, those who wrote down their goals accomplished significantly more than those who did not write down their goals.[1] Who doesn't want to accomplish significantly more?

Every year, before January 1st, I used to write a long list of everything I wanted to accomplish in the next 365 days. The mistake I made was writing down too many goals so that by August, I'd lose heart when I saw how unsuccessful I'd been in accomplishing my long list. I'd give up on the year and roll all those unfinished goals to the next year . . . and then the next year . . . and then the next. It was a frustrating pattern in which I had set myself up for failure.

What I would later discover is that simplifying my list to perhaps three or four items, instead of twenty-five, made accomplishing my goals much more attainable. With a focused structure, I completed my list and was able to add new goals to the list. The most important takeaway from this lesson was making a habit of writing down my goals in the first place. It doesn't matter how many you write down or how wild your dreams grow, just write them down. Once I had them all written, I was able to prioritize them and finish the most important ones first and then move onto a secondary list.

---

1. Gardner and Albee, "Strategies for Achieving Goals," 266.

Write the vision; make it plain on tablets, so he may run who reads it. (Habakkuk 2:2 NKJV)

Writing down your goals brings hope to life. What do I mean by that? When I was a young girl, I remember laying in my bed for hours dreaming of faraway lands, of how I could help people and make positive changes in the world. My dreams about the future extended to how I envisaged my personal life: the home I would own, the man I would like to marry, work, the children I very much wanted to have, financial accomplishments, and so on.

Even though my young life was very different from the life I imagined in the future, I would write down these dreams, and looking at the list created hope in me an expectation, a faith of what was to come. My list represented the endless possibilities of the direction my life could take. I think many of us have forgotten how to dream. Dreaming and visualizing ourselves accomplishing and achieving great things in our lives and the lives of others generates excitement and *joy* that will overwhelm us. It creates an expectancy of what is to come.

Dr. Caroline Leaf says in her book, *Who Switched Off My Brain*, "When you take time to imagine, all kinds of good chemicals flow in your brain."[2] I believe this is one of the keys to unlocking the *joy* just waiting to bust out of you and me. Filling our schedules with too much to do, too many activities, or all work and no play, robs us of that necessary time to imagine, dream and relax. Even if you have to schedule twenty to thirty minutes to dream and relax, do it. Unlock those dreams and promises you buried deep in your heart. Dream away, and unlock your destiny. Smell the air, call a friend, take a walk, plant a tree in honor of someone, spend time with your family, get a massage, open the door for a complete stranger, put the electronics down and dream!

Many people I meet ask me to pray for them. One of the first questions I ask is, "What is your vision? What are your dreams and goals?" So many reply, "I don't know. I gave up dreaming a long time ago." Others say that they have forgotten how to dream, or they say, "I'm too busy or too old to dream." This is a lie! Since when is there a time limit or age limit on dreams? Let me ask you a question, what do Lucille Ball, Vera Wang, Judy Dench, Viola Davis, and Julia Child have in common? They all became successful and began fulfilling their dreams when they were way into their forties, and some even later in life. In fact, Julia Childs didn't even learn how to cook until she was thirty-six. So, dream, stay proactive in life, not reactive,

2. Leaf, *Who Switched Off My Brain*, 43.

purpose to remain *joy*fully curious, pray, never give up hope, and keep believing. Here are some quotes from one of the greatest women comedians of all time who blazed a trail before there was one:

> I'm not funny, what I am is brave. (Lucille Ball)

> I'm happy that I have brought laughter because I have been shown by many the value of it in so many lives, in so many ways. (Lucille Ball)

Reconsider the habitual actions in your life that are not bearing fruit, perhaps leaving you hopeless and *joy*less. Is the consumption of social media reaping a positive influence in your life? Are you taking too many selfies? Is being a workaholic good for you? Is partying all the time fulfilling you? I raise all these questions because if our habits are turning us into insular people who are self-centered, we are robbed of seeing others, which then robs us of *joy*. Selflessness is a much more fulfilling proposition. There is so much *joy*, #*IJOY*, when we give to others, do for others, and give our time to help others. It's free, so try it!

> For it is in giving that we receive. (Saint Francis of Assisi)

Time magazine has an intriguing article about happiness:

> Scientific research provides compelling data to support the anecdotal evidence that giving is a powerful pathway to personal growth and lasting happiness. Through fMRI technology, we now know that giving activates the same parts of the brain that are stimulated by food and sex. Experiments show evidence that altruism is hardwired in the brain—and it's pleasurable. Helping others may just be the secret to living a life that is not only happier but also healthier, wealthier, more productive, and more meaningful.[3]

Wow, isn't that powerful? As I said earlier, giving, helping others, and doing kind acts for people, is actually more powerful than the euphoria we feel from our favorite slice of hot fudge chocolate cake, or even sex! Giving to others brings us *joy*, #*IJOY*. Instead of concentrating your thoughts on what you can get, how about turning that into, "What can I give?"

> "In my life I used to ask what can I get and how much? Now I ask what can I give, and how much." (Brenda Epperson-Moore)

---

3. Santi, "Secret to Happiness."

You may be the type of person that is a natural giver. I know some people who give so selflessly that they have nothing left for themselves. Unless you are Mother Teresa, this can be tricky. I believe life is also about balance. When we give to the extent of neglecting ourselves, our health, our families, finances, and work, the imbalance can lead to severe deficits in life. The very thing that is supposed to bring us *joy* steals our *joy* without the proper balance. Some people cannot remember the last time they gave anyone anything. Clearly, there's an imbalance there.

Which leads me to share with you how important I believe it is to be determined to have *joy, #IJOY*. Don't forget, earlier I shared with you how we are *all* born with *joy*? It's our birthright! We must be determined to maintain and practice being *joyful*, or *joy-filled*, about each and every day. Did you wake up this morning? Then *be* thankful, *be joyful*. Staying connected to God the Father, His son Jesus, and the Holy Spirit is a part of remaining plugged into that *joy* which is the fruit of the Holy Spirit. By daily crucifying our flesh, we are accepting the change that God wants to bring into our lives.

Looking back at my childhood, it was difficult on some days to find *joy* anywhere. After many years of widowhood and financial hardship, my mother found a wonderful man, remarried again, and found a new *joy*. My stepfather had four children, three of whom were older, and one lived with us while I was finishing high school in Oregon. One day, while clearing out the dishwasher, I got into a heated argument with my stepbrother. I don't remember what it was even about, but the next thing I knew, he grabbed a large knife and began chasing me around the house with it. Looking back I'm not sure what he would do if he caught me, but I was happy I never found out. My loud screams finally summoned my mortified mother's attention. Many days were difficult in our home as addictions, drugs, drinking, and tempers were a part of daily life. Finding *joy* on those days was difficult, but I was determined to keep pressing in to God, to keep dreaming, to keep believing, to keep moving forward, and pressing on toward God and my goals. I kept very busy in high school playing tennis, singing, traveling with our high school jazz group, student council, leadership, our church events, and programs, giving of my time, working on the farm or in the veterinarian's office, pageants, and anything else I could get my hands into. These activities kept my heart and mind healthy, helping me to never lose sight of my hopes and dreams for the future, even though keeping that vision alive was oftentimes difficult.

I survived my stepbrother's knife threats, and later on, he apologized for his actions. I had already forgiven him, but he still carried around the guilt of that day. I hugged him, told him to let the incident go, and live freely. His chilling confession to me later—about what he probably would have done with the knife if he had caught me—made me thank God for protecting me.

> I never met a bitter person who was thankful. (Nick Vujicic)

What about illness or physical challenge? There is a man who I believe exemplifies *joy*, *#IJOY*, overcoming obstacles, and breaking all barriers. His name is Nick Vujicic. He has an organization called "Life without Limbs."

> God can use life without limbs to show the world how to live life without limits. (Nick Vujicic)

Nick was born with no arms or legs. He has had to overcome the impossible and even the unthinkable. He is a messenger of hope, telling others about God's love. Nick is the hands and feet of Christ, being used mightily without any limbs. He has been to over sixty-three countries, telling others his story of how he found *joy* even though his physical body was lacking basically everything most people take for granted. He has refused to wallow in self-pity or use his situation as an excuse for bitterness. If he can have *joy* and be used so mightily, what's our excuse? I think, perhaps, this is one of my favorite quotes of all time.

> If you can't get a miracle, become one. (Nick Vujicic)

When the middle of my three daughters was a little girl, she would become so filled with *joy* when she held her warm, fluffy, favorite pink blanket. She would look at me while squeezing her blanket as hard as she could, clenching her teeth together tightly, and say, "Oh Mommy, I just love my Wankie." She would become so overwhelmed with *joy* that she could hardly contain herself. It was just the absolute cutest thing to watch, as this uncontainable *joy*, *#IJOY*, ran through her body like a current.

My oldest daughter expressed her happiness quite differently. She would dance around, smiling and twirling until she fell to the ground. As she landed on her back, her laughter and *joy*, *#IJOY*, spewed out uncontrollably. My youngest daughter is similar to me and did exactly what I used to do when the "*joy* wave," as I call it, would come upon her. She would run through the house and scream in the loudest, most shrill scream imaginable. She was so overcome with *joy*. She said the same thing my mom told me I used to say, as I ran through the house as a kid. My mom would ask me, "Brenda, when you run through the house screaming in excitement, what do you feel? Was it because of a thought you had? Was it something that made you excited that you were thinking about or looking forward to?" "Nope," I would exclaim (just the same words my youngest daughter would say to me), "Sometimes I feel so much *joy* and excitement that I just need to let it out and scream!" That is how I believe we should all live. We need to allow that feeling, the "*joy* wave," to fill us so completely that we want to explode with *joy*. Not because of our outward circumstances, but because we are plugged into, or connected to, the *One* who unlocks the fullness of *joy* in us, #*IJOY*.

I'd like to encourage and challenge you to take time today to dream again, write down your goals and hopes for the future, change the habits that are damaging and unfulfilling to your life, stop, look, and see the beauty in humility and selflessness, recognize the value of others, and never forget, "It is in giving that we receive."

Prayer

As we keep our eyes fixed on you Lord, release us from fear, expand our borders and territory beyond what we see, heal us, and remind us who we are in you, oh Lord. Give us dreams and visions that are in alignment with your word and your will. Let us be quick to forgive ourselves and others, which leads to a steadfast peace. Lead us not into temptation, but deliver us from evil. Thy will be done on earth as it is in heaven.

Challenge Questions

1. When was the last time you purposely gave someone something that brought them *joy*?

2. What was it that brought you *joy*?

3. How did it make you feel? How did it make the others feel?

4. Did what you gave that person add value to their life? Did it change their life in some way?

5. Write down three dreams that are so radical it would blow you and everyone away if they happened. At least one of these things should be to help others. Now sit, wait, pray, and take time to visualize and dream of these things coming to pass.

8

Hurry Up So You Can Slow Down

THERE IS A REAL art to relaxing and slowing down. Especially these days with the fast pace of life, the internet, a growing to-do list, emails, and texts that never seem to be complete. I don't know about you, but in my house now, as well as growing up, summertime was when life slowed down. We would, on purpose, just lay in bed some days late into the morning hours. We would have a barbeque and invite friends over we hadn't seen for a while, take long walks, go to the beach, sit and read a book, or do house projects we had been putting off. So many of us have forgotten how to relax or even slow down.

Upon graduating from High school, I felt a new sense of accomplishment. Not only had I graduated and felt so fulfilled, but it felt so empowering because I finally had a report card with more A's than ever before. In the years past, I was mostly a C-average student, only getting A's in music and physical education. It seemed as though everything was finally falling into place. All of my hard work and prayers were paying off, and I was experiencing success in areas of my life that seemed stagnant. I entered a pageant, won, and was crowned Miss Oregon United Teenager. This, of course, didn't happen on the first, try or even the second, but remember, if you are passionate about something, if at first, you don't succeed try, try, try again.

You never fail until you stop trying. (Albert Einstein)

Being crowned Miss Oregon United Teenager was an incredible sense of accomplishment for me. Especially since I had to overcome my fears of standing on a stage in a bathing suit. Yikes! There is so much power in overcoming fear rather than allowing fear to overcome you. Winning this pageant made me feel as though I could accomplish anything, my dreams were actually unfolding and coming to life for the first time! I was voted Vice President of my high school student body. I went to state finals in tennis. I was selected as lead vocalist in one of the high school jazz group competitions. I began to try out for and compete in anything I could get my hands on—that I was passionate about—with relentless pursuit. This helped me overcome some of my fears and insecurities and opened up a new door for me to just love *me* exactly where I was. This realization gave me the strength to push ahead, push through fears, and try new things. Every single time I tried something new that was of interest to me, I learned something, I grew, I overcame, I was challenged, and realized I had more in me to give than I ever realized.

> We all have obstacles. The feeling of satisfaction comes by overcoming something. (Marta)

The summer after high school graduation, the realization began to hit me that I was leaving this small town in Oregon and never coming back just like my mother had said. At least I would never be back to live there again. Although growing up in a small town was nice, California was calling, or rather screaming, my name. I couldn't wait to get back to the sun, the beaches, hustle and bustle, endless career and creative opportunities, and finally start my life.

I wasn't sure about attending college, but I did finally get accepted into a small college in Orange County called SCC. I was over the moon about all the possibilities that lie ahead, not to mention how close the beach was to the proximity to the college! California ocean here I come! I loaded up my luggage and my parents drove me down to sunny California. This new life suited me well, college, beach, tennis, friends, the hot sun instead of the Oregon liquid sun . . . and dates. When I say dates, I'm not talking about the kind you eat, I had a date with a new guy almost every night! This was definitely new for me. Looking back there was something so magical about the eighties. There was such a feeling of freedom and a little innocence still left in the world. What a fun time college was for me! I even got a part-time job at the preschool down the street to pay for my food and frequent trips to the flea market on the weekends. I didn't have a car, so I would ride my bike to the preschool and work with the kids for after-school programs they set up to keep the kids busy and motivated. I absolutely loved working with these children. The principal came up to me and said she was amazed at how I was able to transition into the steps of the prior leader. The principal was shocked at how well the kids responded to me and actually listened to me when I'd ask them to do something.

Halfway through my first year of college, I received a letter from the school stating that my tuition hadn't been paid through the rest of the year. Shocked, I called my parents and they shared the devastating news that they didn't have the money they thought they would to take care of my tuition through the rest of the year. They had tried to get extensions and loans, but were unable. My dad's business took a turn for the worse and he wasn't able to keep up. Frozen, I wasn't sure what I was going to do. Do I try to take out a loan? Do I try to get another job? No option seemed to cover the huge looming college bill I would acquire to finish paying off the rest of my semester if I stayed. Upon much thinking and praying, I quickly realized the last thing I wanted to do was incur a huge amount of debt at such a young age. Besides, loans take a while to get, and the school wanted their money now. Sadly, I packed up my room, my bags, said goodbye to all my new friends, and left broken-hearted back to Oregon. Not wanting to make my parents feel any worse than they already did, I quietly cried half of the long drive back to Oregon. What would my future hold? How could God work anything good in this? What does this mean for my future?

Upon arriving back to Oregon which had always been a wonderful home to me, I welcomed the smells of the new home my parents had moved into during the time I was at school. We now lived in Salem, which is the capital of Oregon. It was a much larger town than Dallas, Oregon, where I grew up, which made me feel a bit better. There were more opportunities, as well as jobs, so I thought to myself, "Maybe I could get back on my feet quickly, make some money, figure out plan B, and then head back down to California, for in my heart, that was the only place for me." So once again, I began to pray, set my goals, make my lists, write them all down, and dream big, and in keeping with my goals, I applied for a waitressing job. I know that sounds weird, but I knew this was the quickest cash-on-hand job that allowed me flexibility in my day. I still hadn't gotten my first credit card yet, so cash was the way to go. I became very disciplined and saved as much money as I possibly could. As for the waitress's life? It didn't take me long to realize I wasn't a very good waitress. I liked meeting new people but at times I'd forget part of an order, or I had so many people in my station that I couldn't get to some tables as quickly as they wanted and that didn't make them happy, we all know when people are hungry their patience begins wearing thin.

At one point in my day, a huge party entered the restaurant and filled my section. I panicked a bit. Feverishly, I ran back and forth, got the orders, got the drinks, the bread, water, and menus. Now keep in mind this was basically a diner, so I didn't have busboys helping me pour water and collect things. I was it! While squeezing through the small isles of people holding the food and soup high above everyone, I accidentally dropped dribbles of soup on a customer's head. On his bald head! Yikes! He yelled loudly, and I immediately stopped and just froze. Everyone at the table stopped talking. All eyes were on me. I was standing there, hot soup in my hand, and all I could do at that point was apologize profusely for my mishap. I didn't know if I should take a napkin to wipe it off his head or just leave it, so awkwardly I left it. This didn't go over well with my boss as he already had to comp a few meals I messed up that day. Let's suffice it to say I didn't last very much longer there.

The following year a few of my college friends got an apartment and needed a fourth person to live with them, and they asked me. I was all in! Living in Oregon wasn't fulfilling my longing for the vast opportunities in the entertainment business, singing, the California sun, and sand. I loaded up my little Plymouth Champ again and drove back down to California. I needed a job to pay my part of the rent and fast, so my friend looked into getting me a job at the insurance company she worked at. I thought I would try this office thing to see if it was something I was interested in or even cut out for. All the while Hollywood was screaming my name. I kept telling myself to just try this office corporate stuff for one year, and hey, maybe you'll like the corporate world. My friend inquired at her insurance company and was confident she could get me in for the new job opening. It didn't take me long to realize being a secretary wasn't even kind of in my skill set. I almost got fired so many times. I couldn't type (back then we had typewriters, not computers and word processing), and half the time I would give my work to my friend, Brenda, who got me the job. She would oftentimes have to type and finish my work for me. There was only so much white-out one could use on a letter, and my boss required no mistakes on his letters that were sent out.

After a year of what felt like torture and almost getting fired on numerous occasions, I finally quit. Once again, I was crying and driving on the long road back to Oregon, disillusioned, tired, and feeling bad about my lack of being able to move toward my dreams. As a matter of fact, I was going in the opposite direction. Once again my home state of Oregon welcomed me back with open arms. I went back to waitressing, dreaming, and praying . . . hard. I began to ask God what *His* plan for my life was and how I could partner with him to fulfill my dreams of singing, traveling the world, changing and reaching people's lives. My sister, who was crowned Miss Oregon USA, received a call from a past associate who asked her if she would be interested in traveling abroad with a group of beauty queens and actors. My sister couldn't take the time off work to travel so she referred me. This was an incredible opportunity, I interviewed and was chosen to travel to Thailand to sing and headline at different events with other dancers, this incredible opportunity allowed us to travel all over the country. I was elated and scared all at the same time. In my heart, I knew this was an incredible opportunity, but I also knew, in the eighties, safety was certainly an issue. Again, I chose to *Rise Up* out of fear and walk through that open door.

Traveling abroad for the first time was an experience of a lifetime. I sang for the King and Queen of Thailand, dignitaries, and learned a culture I had never known before. Prior to leaving on this trip, I remember my mother looked at me and said, "Once you leave you will never be the same when you arrive home. You won't be able to remain here in this sleepy town. God will open your eyes to a whole new world." She was so right. I connected with the Thai people in a deep way; their kindness, warm hearts, and culture catapulted me into a new way of thinking. I saw myself and the world differently.

One evening while at a nightclub in downtown Bangkok I met a girl from the Philippines who shared her story with me, of how she endured abuse back at home, she explained this would be the last trip she was to take as a single girl. I inquired for a deeper explanation, and she explained that in her family and much of her country, she wasn't allowed to pick her husband or even the time when she was to be married. Her parents arranged the marriage for her. I asked her, "What about love?" She said it wasn't about love; her family was forcing her to marry this man. Chills ran down my spine as she spoke. The memory of this conversation will be forever etched in my mind while the loud music was pulsating in the background as tears flowed from her eyes facing an uncertain future. Speaking with her gave me a new appreciation for my life, my home, and my country.

With a whole new perspective on life, I arrived home from Thailand and quickly got a job singing at a club in the evenings. After I got off work waitressing, my intention was to save money and move back to Los Angeles, I was no longer fulfilled in a smaller environment. A friend of mine, Ardi, allowed me to stay in her place in the city so I could be closer to my waitressing day job. While living with her, I would mention my faith and share with her all that God had done for me. She let me know that the faith and church stuff wasn't for her, all the while she still allowed me to stay on her couch. She was a single mother, looking back when I think of how generous she was, I am overwhelmed by her kindness. God worked on both of our lives while I lived there.

One day God moved in a mighty way, I was able to share my faith with her not by talking, but by living. What I mean by that is I didn't stand there preaching at her or telling her what was wrong or right, I simply lived my faith out loud. I would say things like, "I am praying for you," or when she would walk in the room and ask what I'm doing, I would say, "I'm reading my Bible." God used it all to silently speak to her heart even when I wasn't aware of it. I'll never forget when she came to me, tears streaming down her face and exclaimed she gave her heart to the Lord. The softness that came over her was astounding; it was like a blanket of love had overtaken her heart and totally transformed her from the inside out. It was so wonderful to be able to witness and share God's love with my friend, who is actually now out in the world doing some missionary work because of how God transformed her life. Wow, now that's bearing fruit.

I love that saying if you're not where you want to be, bloom where you are planted. Little by little I began to book modeling or speaker jobs through the local talent agency in Portland, which paid way more money than waitressing. I saved money and ultimately was able to set a date to move back down to California, this time with a long-time family friend whom I called 'aunt.' She had recently been widowed and welcomed having a girl in her home as she had raised four boys. Once again, I loaded up my car and drove back down to California right smack dab in the heart of Hollywood to finally pursue my dreams of singing. While driving on the long, hot I-5 Freeway, I kept praying and saying to myself, "I want my life to be an example of hope, leadership, and purpose." I wanted to be a person of action, truth and commitment, a person God and others could depend upon. During my drive down, Aunt Marge had a heart attack. I was so sad and worried for her. When I spoke to my mother, I was devastated. Not only for her, but I also realized I was going to have to turn around and come back to Oregon. She couldn't possibly want me to come live with her now. Thank

God for her love and kindness. The opposite was true, and over the phone she said she wouldn't have it any other way. I got to her house in Southern California, moved all of my clothes into my room, which I gladly shared with my aunt, and began beating the streets working on my singing career.

I entered the Miss California USA pageant and placed in the top-ten. I won best in swimsuit, which was a HUGE feat for me as I struggled with my self-esteem and my weight. Being a part of Miss California USA was an incredible experience. I learned so much about myself and saw that the only obstacles in my way were the ones I didn't face. I also entered a few other pageants and placed in the top-ten.

While pageants were a wonderful opportunity, I realized it wasn't a path for me. These opportunities changed my life and showed me how many infinite possibilities were out there waiting for me to grab. I found a great church to attend, called "Church on the Way." I got a commercial agent, worked on my music in Los Angeles, and began to knock on any door that would open. I was the thinnest I had ever been, or really could ever be for my body type, yet when I went into the modeling agencies, they'd weigh me and say, "Yes you are the right weight, but you look too athletic. You need to look even thinner. You have to much muscle." I thought, "You've got to be kidding me?" I was more frustrated, a little sad, but mostly annoyed. I finally found an agency that took me on, but that didn't last long. I was hungry all the time and quickly realized back then that my natural athletic build wasn't suited for modeling. Whether it was acting, commercials, modeling, or any agencies, some agents would say, you're too tall, too heavy, too blonde, too pretty, change your nose, color your hair, and on and on and on and on. The one common denominator they all would say was, "You've got a lot of talent." Not much consolation, but I held onto those words, my faith, and constant drive.

All that criticism took a toll on me. I began to believe that I wasn't good enough the way I was. It's amazing how we listen and believe the lies others say.

> I'm not upset that you lied to me, I'm upset that from now on I can't believe you. (Friedrich Nietzsche)

Unfortunately, I began to believe the lie. Food and I began a horrible relationship. I worked out three to four hours a day—morning then in the afternoon—religiously. The cycle became too intense. I was eating less and less growing thinner and thinner. Even though I was already so thin, when

I looked in the mirror, all I saw was that fat little girl who was mercilessly teased every day in grade school. I booked some modeling jobs, and at one point, they wanted me to fly to another country to work overseas. Too many unknown variables for me, and in my heart and spirit I knew God had a big door for me that He wanted to open right here in the good 'ole US of A.

Suddenly, I stopped my monthly cycle. Worried, I went to the doctor, and he said, "If you don't start eating more, and getting more nutrition, you will become sterile, and you won't be able to conceive children." That was all I needed to hear. Food here I come! Then, of course, you guessed it, I began to eat and eat and eat and eat; then, I was back to overeating again. I'll never forget my all-time low was when I snuck out of my aunt's house, after midnight, probably around 1 am, all alone walking, to the 24-hour store to get snacks. I bought the snacks and ate them by myself sitting under a streetlight at 2 am. What was I thinking? How did I care so little about myself that I would put myself in this kind of danger or harm for food? What was this really about? After eating everything in my hands, I began to cry. I didn't recognize myself anymore. I made it back safely that morning, fell on my knees, and asked God for help, clarity, and strength.

Day by day, God breathed new life into my heart and soul. One day, while sitting with my sister and best friend, Tim, my sister asked me a pointed question which I will never forget. She asked, "What happened to you, Brenda? Something must have happened. You are not yourself. You are so angry, you basically don't even like men, you have so much anger and pain, you are not yourself." Then she said, "Did someone hurt you when you were young? Did someone violate you?" I don't know what it was about that moment or the questions she asked, but it was as if someone had unlocked a secret place that began to flood through my head with memories that began to rush through my mind and soul. Then, a tidal wave of emotions burst through my brain and heart as I exploded in tears. I was finally letting go. Finally revealing that secret that I kept locked deep inside, buried away so nobody would know. Little did I know that I was living my pain out loud. What I thought was hidden was visible to others. Knowing I was in a safe place with Tim and Deborah, I began to sob uncontrollably in this small restaurant. My sister said, "I knew it. I knew something happened." I began to unravel all the years of my shame and sorrow. I began to tell them the story of when the neighborhood boy pulled me behind the couch in my own home and raped me. Through the tears, as I told them the story and details, the bondage of shame and anger began to loosen off of me, the dark black veil was lifted from my heart and soul as truth, freedom, and *joy* flooded through my veins once again. In a short period of time the heaviness was gone. It's as though, once again, that same God-like electric shock of love ran through my body that I felt as a young girl when I gave my heart to Christ. I was instantly healed of the years of bondage that had been trying to hold me down and lie to me.

> Bring me your hurting heart, I'll mend all the broken parts, together we'll get through it, live through it love one another then healing starts. (Brenda Epperson-Moore and Tim Miner, "Healing Starts")

Over time, many prayers, and pressing into God, I also shed the unhealthy relationship I had with food. It's amazing how when we believe in a lie, bondage soon follows. I believed I wasn't thin enough. I believed I was bad, dirty, used, unloved, unworthy, and unloveable from the rape. Both of those incidents almost stole my whole life, but God has radically changed and healed me, and He can heal you too!

Prayer

Dear God, help us love ourselves the way you love us. Help us to see you. Even in my biggest life mistakes, I know I am not a mistake. You have a purpose for me to be here on this earth. Help me in my unbelief and turn it into flaming arrows of hope for such a time as this.

Challenge Questions

1. What lie are you believing? What can you do today to reverse your thinking and move forward in hope and in truth of how Christ sees you? Read Romans 8:1–3.

2. What words have people spoken over you that you have to remove from your heart and mind? Write the words down and see how ridiculous they are. Leave them on the paper and never allow them another moment of space in your soul.

3. What is one thing you have always wanted to do, but haven't done?

4. When is the last time you did something just for you just for fun?

5. Make a plan, write down one step toward your goals of freedom and begin to encourage yourself in the Lord today.

9

Ready Or Not Here I Come

IT'S SO EASY TO forget how precious life is as the clock continuously ticks and moments slip away; if we blink, we lose another precious moment. That's why it is so important to live each day, explore new opportunities, try new things, and take small and big chances in life. I'll never forget when I tried out for my high school play, which was the acclaimed Broadway theatrical play, *Oliver*. I was hopeful as I tried out for one of the female leads, and since I was so passionate about singing, this was right up my alley. I'll never forget how nervous and exhilarating I was all at the same time, having to remember and then recite lines in front of my teacher and peers. It was at that moment, I promised myself that I would not sit on the sidelines of life and watch it go by. I would always take risks in life, whether they paid off or not. The next day, I received news that I got a part in the play, but not the part I had hoped for; nope, I had landed the mean old lady Mrs. Sowerberry. I was a little stunned as I began to read this character's description. Mrs. Sowerberry was a mean, old, crotchety woman, and I felt she was the antithesis of me. What was my theatre teacher thinking casting me in this role? Then I realized what a great opportunity it was to expand the boundaries I had set up in my mind, to go beyond how I saw myself, and stretch my potential in an entirely different direction.

Sometimes God does that with us. We may see ourselves going in one direction when all of a sudden God pulls the rug out from under us so we can look at life from an entirely new view that we otherwise wouldn't have seen. Waiting for the perfect timing or conditions leads to inactivity. Each experience or chance we take builds on the next. Taking chances and risks allows us to grow beyond the limitations we have set for ourselves. Taking risks helps us become more confident and stretches us to reach more people.

Take courage, explore, grab hold of an opportunity or an open door, and move forward in hope. Hope is the silver lining to your dark cloud. We don't hope in the world because the world is subject to greed, division, change, and confusion. We hope in God. Hope is the sun breaking through the storm, lighting up a darkened sky in our hearts and lives.

> God is limitless. He is bigger than the box we put him in therefore, the only limits we have are the limits we put on God and ourselves. (Brenda Epperson-Moore)

Do you believe in miracles? Sometimes a miracle is in short supply, sometimes we forget all God has done for us and we need to remember just breathing is a miracle and actually miracles happen every day. This day was one such day. I had moved from Oregon to Hollywood, which seemed to be calling me. I went to every casting office that would let me in to drop off pictures and resume. I beat the streets until they bled, or at least until my feet did. My daily ritual was: I woke up, worked out, waitressed, auditioned, worked out again, and then the next day started all over. I had this passion and drive to leave my mark on the world and Hollywood. I had this burning desire in me to reach for the limitless creativity opportunities afforded to me in Hollywood. Practically every day I read my Bible, prayed, and asked God to show me the way, to put me at the right place at the right time, to give me favor—and a job! I found a good church to anchor my soul in and began to trust and fall into the arms of God in a way I had only done as a young girl.

As a starving singer and actress, landing a job at a nearby seafood restaurant was just what I needed to get by. I was still making payments on a beautiful car that I loved when one day while my car was parked on the street, someone plowed into my car and thrust it into the neighbor's yard two doors down. You guessed it, not much of my car was left but it was still drivable, and as a starving singer/actress, I couldn't afford to fix it, so I hopped back into my badly damaged, rickety car and drove it slowly home. I felt embarrassed as my trunk was now in my back seat and the noises it made were rather loud and scary. Trying to hold back the tears and look at the bright side, I was thankful that this new waitress job allowed me more work hours which meant more tips and more money. Perhaps I could afford to fix the damage. I took every extra shift so I could to earn enough money to potentially buy a new car. One day I walked out to my car, turned the key, and nothing, my engine didn't turn over and my car wouldn't budge. How can I afford to tow my car to the auto shop? I called a nearby place and asked them how much It would cost to fix my car. I explained the situation and the guy just laughed, looked at me, and said, "It's worth scraps only. I'll give you $100." Feeling frustrated and late for my shift at the restaurant, I grabbed my bike and rode to work and auditions that were close enough to where I lived. I felt like a failure, I felt humiliated and felt as though I sunk to a new low. How would I afford a new car? I needed a break and fast. My parents were struggling financially and couldn't help, I was barely paying my rent, and now, no car.

I called my agents and said, with a begging tone in my voice, "Don't you have any work for me? There must be something I would be right for?" Eureka! There was a commercial my agent said that I would be perfect for; it was for Toshiba, and I was a "party girl" All I had to do was stand in a group of people in a beautiful sequin dress and dance around. You can imagine at the audition I poured it on thick, and through the miraculous hand of God, I booked it! I finally had a paycheck; the job was fun and confusing all at the same time.

While on the commercial shoot the producers motioned over to me, thinking I was in trouble. I walked over and said, "Yes," thinking, "Oh, please don't fire me." They actually pulled me out of the group to then have me "showcase" their new Toshiba computer. I was thrilled to be noticed. I sat with the computer on my lap smiled as they filmed me as the camera zoomed in closer and closer. They then asked me, in broken English, to type on the computer keyboard and smile. I thought that can't be hard until they started zooming in on my nails! Yikes, I had no money and couldn't afford to get my acrylic nails done before the shoot. You guessed it, I had broken and chipped nails, some completely off my fingers. I was mortified. The next thing I remember is the director and producers all started crowding around me speaking in Japanese pointing at my hands making very loud noises of disgust and unbelief. Not knowing what they were saying I quickly said, "Look I can just use these fingers." Naturally, I chose the fingers that still had fingernails on them. They paused, looked at me, and with a wave, motioned the filming to proceed. I learned a very valuable lesson that day: just like Coach John Wooden explained, when opportunity knocks, we need to be 100 percent prepared even in the smallest of details because the small details *DO* matter. This was also an invaluable lesson in breaking barriers, boundaries, and roadblocks I had set in my mind. Never having acted and not thinking I could do it, those naysayer voices began to quiet in my head. Maybe I could do more than I ever thought possible?

> If you hear a voice within you say you cannot paint, then by all means paint and that voice will be silenced. (Vincent van Gogh)

When the doors of the restaurant closed, I was back looking for more waitressing work. I had a thought about being more strategic as to where I work; after all, if I worked at a random restaurant, there wasn't as much of a chance for me to "get noticed." They had a commissary there and where all of the producers, directors, and executives would head down for lunch. This was the perfect place to meet people and possibly book more work I thought. I actually landed a few jobs while working at MGM. I was chosen as a game show host for a new TV pilot and chosen by the CEO of the building to become Ms. Filmland, I wasn't sure what it meant or what my tasks were, but there were some great articles and promotions that came my way because of this job. Things were looking up. I then started working evenings at MGM/Filmland, waitressing at their events, which gave me double the cash in my pocket to help pay gas, food, and rent.

I had no idea how my life would change on this particular day that I went into work at MGM during the evening's event. This was an event in which soap opera stars were modeling. From the day I stepped foot into Hollywood, I would hear over and over again that I looked like an actress on CBS daytime soap opera, *The Young and the Restless*. There she was, that very same actress walking down the runway at this fundraiser I was waitressing at. I'll never forget what happened next: the manager of the restaurant came to me with a glass of champagne in his hands; I looked at him inquisitively as I wasn't sure if he was offering me the champagne or what was exactly happening. With food stains all over me and my brow filled with sweat since we were working hard that evening, I was perplexed as my manager handed me the champagne. Was I going on a break? He looked at me and said, "There is that girl on *The Young and the Restless*, that everyone says you look like. Go backstage and give her this champagne and introduce yourself. Maybe she can help you." I was stunned and quickly blurted, "What about all of my tables?" He said, "I'll take over your tables for you. Don't worry about it. Go and say hi to her." I was stunned but happy to get a little break. So, I walked backstage and saw the girl who so many people mistook me for. Sweating from running around and bussing my tables, I shyly introduced myself and handed her the champagne. I told her the story of how everyone constantly asks me for her autograph, thinking I was her. We kind of looked at each other to see if we saw the similarities, and at that moment, yet another miracle occurred. She said to me, "You know, I'm not going to be renewing my contract with CBS, and they are going to be looking for another 'Ashley' replacement character. You should audition for the part." I was stunned, and I immediately said, "Sure I'd like that." She gave me her phone number, and we waved goodbye. I carried that piece of paper in my apron pouch like it was a treasured gem.

In the days to follow, I sought God on my knees and cried out for a miracle. I realized this was a huge opportunity, and I must act quickly, so I took a deep breath and called the CBS casting office directly, not having an acting agent. This was unprecedented, I was told time and time again by others, "You can't do it this way. This isn't the way things are done." Sometimes God is looking for us to break out of our small box and step out in faith so we can bust open the doors of change. With butterflies in my stomach and a prayer on my tongue, I began leaving messages at the CBS casting office stating that I would like to audition for the role of Ashley on *The Young and the Restless.* Back in the day before our lives were run by computers, I relentlessly sent my 8x10 headshots and resume via the post office into casting offices and studios. I had only a commercial agent at the time, and with no formal training or even an agent to represent me, I boldly walked through the door set before me. I am a big believer in walking through a door once it's open—ready or not here I come. I kept saying, "If you opened this door, God, you must think I'm ready to walk through it, even though I have no clue as to what I am doing."

Then it happened. While walking through my apartment living room one day, my phone rang. I answered and couldn't believe my ears. The voice of the casting director from CBS was calling. They finally called me and invited me in for an audition! I was stunned. What a mighty God we serve. Naturally, I was shaking in my boots not even knowing what to expect, never having walked into a major network casting office. Did I forget to mention that the seafood restaurant job I had closed their doors, and now, I had no job, no car, and no prospects of work ahead? I called my family and asked for a special prayer covering, grabbed my headshots, and asked a friend to drive me to CBS for my "go see." That basically means we want to see you in person before we commit to actually giving you an audition. Before walking into the office, I tried to anticipate any questions I would be asked. One of them I knew would be for certain, "What acting classes have you been taking?" I had no money left so there was definitely not enough money to pay for acting classes. Crafty as I was, before I walked into the office, I got the names of a few acting coaches in town so I could rattle their names off. The hallway seemed to swallow me up as the endless photos of famous actors and TV shows made me feel smaller as I moved toward the elevator that may or may not carry a part of my new destiny. "It's a door, Brenda. It's a door, Brenda." I wish I could say I sprinted through the door, but this time, I crawled through the door sheepishly, not knowing what I was doing. "Just keep walking Brenda," I kept reminding myself.

> I have placed before you an open door that no one can shut.
> (Revelation 3:8 NIV)

I arrived at the CBS office trying not to show my fear and was greeted by a kind receptionist which took the edge off my fear. Palms sweating, I was called into the casting office, and much to my surprise was met with a bright, warm kind-hearted woman who immediately made me feel welcome. Our conversion moved quickly into the casting director asking me, "What have you been doing lately? What acting classes have you been taking?" I couldn't possibly tell her my only acting experience was Mrs. Sowerberry in the highschool play, *Oliver*. So, I quickly muttered the names of the local acting coaches I had memorized so I didn't look like a complete idiot. All the while I knew if I could just get my foot in the door, God would do the rest.

The meeting went longer than I imagined, and the outcome better than I could have ever anticipated. I left holding a script and "sides," which are the lines my character would speak; I also landed a second interview. Hooray, now what? I literally had no clue how to break down a script and act. I kept thinking, "If I could just sing the role it would be so much easier." That didn't happen, so I called as many friends as I possibly could and asked them if they knew of any cheap acting coaches who could help me learn how to act, fast, or was there such a thing? My confidence wavered as, once again, I fell on my knees and asked God to make a way where there didn't seem to be one. Almost daily, my prayer consisted of "Help."

Miracles do happen, a phone call came through from a friend stating she knew of an acting coach who could help me learn and breakdown my character lines. The pressure was on as I only had one week until my next big audition. I would sit on my couch and spend hours reading and memorizing my lines and trying my best to learn how to act. I only had enough money for two private acting coach lessons so I had to squeeze every bit of knowledge from him that I could. Upon finishing my second and final lesson, he looked at me and said, "You need more training." I explained to him I had no money left, and it was either the frantic look on my face or my horrible acting that led him to agree to help me one more time for free. Another miracle had happened. Thank God for another open door!

> Our prayers should be for blessings in general, for God knows best
> what is good for us. (Socrates)

The day came that I walked through the doors of CBS once again. I sat in the familiar casting office and delivered my lines with as much confidence and purpose as I could muster. When I was done, the casting director looked at me and said, "That was pretty good." I almost fainted. She said, "Here take this scene, memorize it and come back again next week." I thought I was in a dream and asked her to repeat herself. I left the office feeling as though a mighty force from heaven had pushed me into a new vision for my life that I had never considered. After all, I moved to LA to sing, not to act, but here I was now auditioning a third time for a lead on a top-five television soap opera I had never even watched before. My planning and hard work seemed to pay off.

As I walked back through those halls, I couldn't help but stop, and look at the wildly successful actors and shows that had gone before me. Shows like *Carol Burnett, Magnum, P.I., The Nanny, Everybody Loves Raymond,* on and on. I began to see myself on that wall. "Why not me," I thought to myself. Remember, there is a place for each of us not only in God's kingdom, but in the work He predestined and planned for us if we dare to keep walking through those doors. Miracles still happen today; God uniquely uses each person to accomplish His purpose, not only for your life, but for the lives of those you will then touch.

With a skip in my step and a new bulldog determination I pressed into God and my new script with new vigor, and since I had almost run out of money and still had no job and no car, I placed all my focus on this new shiny door God had opened before me. I had come to realize in life that if we have an open door, the perfect conditions may not be in existence, and we may not even be fully ready, but walk through the door anyway, and do it afraid if you need to! Another week went by and another meeting with the casting office, and this time with producers also. My nerves seemed to break as I could hardly catch my breath thinking of auditioning in front of producers this time. The day came for me to walk back down those hall-ways of CBS Television Studios. Every day I walked more confidently and understood that this could have only happened by the grace and power of God. Walking into the producer's office, I felt as though I had six-hundred pound weights on my legs. Three people were staring at me, and the greet-ing was not warm. As I read the scene with the casting director, I saw in her eyes that she was almost rooting for me. I could tell she was in my corner and wanted me to succeed.

In the days to follow, I waited eagerly by the phone, anticipating a call. Day after day came, and my heart grew heavier and heavier realizing that maybe it was over. I kept telling myself God's approval is enough. I don't need the approval of man. God is for me, and if God is for me then who can be against me? The days turned into weeks. No phone call. No message on my machine. My heart became heavy and my wallet empty. God, I need a miracle and a job!

Prayer

God you have called us all to be fearLESS in life. Help us to be bold in our thinking to trust you, to take a giant leap of faith; even if we fall, you will help us get back up again. You said in your word that if we have faith as small as a mustard seed, we can say to a mountain, "move," and it will move. You can take what little we have to offer to you and multiply it into something supersized. When I am afraid I will worship you. When I cannot see the road ahead, I will trust you. When I am at the end of my rope, I will remain in your steadfast love and peace. I will pray and not panic.

Challenge Questions

1. What do you do when you are faced with a desperate situation? We have a choice: we can choose fear or faith. Switch the channel of your mind to faith. Turn off fear. Write three ways you can do this.

2. If you were faced with an opportunity that you were unprepared for, would you shrink back or walk through those doors boldly? Sometimes we need to do it afraid.

3. I love the definition of Challenge; it is: *A call or dare for someone to compete in a contest or sport.* What is God calling you to complete that you have been delaying? What is one step you can take to begin conquering this challenge?

10

When the Impossible Becomes Possible

You MAY NOT FEEL as though you have unique abilities, or that you are in a position to do anything great for God, but God is great, and He is living on the inside of you, and He is a God of supernatural miracles. He has made us all in His image with unique abilities and purpose. As we trust in God and communicate with Him, that's how we build our relationship and faith in Him. He will ignite a new flame in you that sparks a direction and purpose that will bring a fantastic awakening in your life and maybe even change the world. After all, the definition of a miracle is an event that is not explicable by natural or scientific laws.

Day after day after day went by. No phone call from the studio. I quickly realized it would have to be a miracle for my phone to ring from the CBS casting office. Desperate I called everywhere to find another job. My parents weren't able to help me financially, and I was getting scared as the bills were mounting, my checking account dwindling. It's in these moments I believe Satan attacks us and causes us to freeze with fear and doubt, which then chips away at our faith in God.

Refusing to believe God would bring me this far to leave me destitute, I pressed into prayer and did everything on my end to find a job. My phone began to ring with returned phone calls for possible jobs. Upon answering what I thought was a call for a job, I heard a familiar voice on the other end. I asked, "Hello, Jill is that you?" "Yes," she said. It was Jill Wilson Newton, the casting director from *The Young and the Restless*. I was stunned. Before I could say anything else, she said to me that I was chosen along with three other girls to screen test for the role of Ashley Abbott. I screamed and almost dropped the phone as I leaped into the air almost hitting my head on the ceiling of my apartment. "Thank you, thank you, thank you," I said, over and over again. I'll never forget what she said to me: "I didn't do anything, it was all of your hard work." That meant so much to me. In the days to come the script was mailed to my apartment in an official CBS envelope. I felt as though God had parted the Red Sea for me.

> What would life be if we had no courage to attempt anything?
> (Vincent van Gogh)

Reading the description of the scene and the type of clothes I was to wear shot terror up my spine as the realization sunk in my heart that I had nothing in my closet to wear, so I took the only department store credit card I had and ran to buy business attire for my upcoming screen test. Now imagine me, never having acted a day in my life, and now, I'm screen testing for a major role on a top-three rated soap opera at CBS. This could only be the hand of God. While in the dressing room at the department store, I kept looking at the price tags and thought to myself, "How am I going to pay for this with no job?" Then I thought, "I only have to wear these once," so I did what we sometimes did back then: I bought this beautiful pink blazer and black skirt on credit, tucked in the tags, and then planned to return the clothes after the screen test. I know that sounds bad, but I think we have all done that a time or two in our lives.

Today was the big day of the screen test. I knocked on the door of my neighbor, Morty who kindly offered to drive me to CBS. As I got in his 1960s, rusted-out car in my brand new, way-too-expensive business suit, the moment brought me back to my childhood. There was much *joy* to be found in my childhood but not much financial means. Before my mom married my dad, I have these vivid memories of getting into my mother's old drafty, paint-chipped rusted-out farm truck in which I would always make her pull far away from the school because I was embarrassed to have my peers see me in it. Never having the nerve to tell my mom and possibly hurt her I kept that to myself. This time I wasn't embarrassed being in a rusted dented car. I was thankful to have a ride even in that rusted car, I was thankful that I did not have to walk or ride my bike to the audition at CBS that day. It's amazing how our perspective shifts when we mature and approach things with an attitude of gratitude.

As Morty and I pulled up to CBS Television Studios, sweet eighty-year-old Morty said, "Good luck kid," and drove away. This whole moment just seemed crazy to me; this was way bigger than what I could pull off. I muttered under my breath, "If you don't show up for me God, I'm sunk." I waved to the parking attendant and spoke to the guard as I had made so many trips to CBS by this time, and I knew almost everyone by name. Walking down those long CBS hallways, I was so grateful to be in this position.

When I arrived on the stage floor of the building, Floor 2, I saw huge lights, cameras, and sets, and all of the behind-the-scenes hustle and bustle of filming could be heard and seen. Suddenly, I heard the crowd screaming on the stage across the hall and then the famous Bob Barker saying, "Come on down, you're the next contestant on *The Price is Right.*" "Wow, this place is phenomenal. Am I really here?" I thought to myself. My nerves began to kick in as I walked into the harried makeup room for final touch-ups before being called down to the stage.

While sitting, waiting to be called on stage, and nerves mounting, I met one of the girls trying out for the same part as me. She was so pretty and very polished. She sized me up and quickly began to rattle off her resume, which was impressive, then she asked me what I had done in film and television prior to this. I said, "Uh, nothing really," to which she tilted her head and looked at me with a bit of disgust, and with a blank stare she said, "So, how'd you get here?" I shrugged my shoulders and said, "God, God got me here."

As though it was perfectly timed, I heard my name over the loudspeaker in the makeup room. They called me down for blocking: "Brenda Epperson to stage one for blocking with the director." "Wait, blocking? What's blocking?" I thought to myself. I was met by the director on the set in which the scene was to be played. He then told me where to move and stand when I said certain lines. Blankly staring at him, he said, "Write what I'm telling you in your script." Yikes. I took a deep breath and tried to absorb all of the information that was being thrown at me like rapid-fire.

As I frantically took notes on the script, I thought to myself, "More to learn. How can I remember all of this direction which was so foreign to me?" I thought my head was going to explode and my heart would beat out of my chest from the excitement, fear, and stress, when, all of the sudden, I heard a small voice in my spirit say, "You were meant for this!" "Wow, that's right. I'm more than a conqueror. I'm a singer. I have performed many times under tons of pressure, in front of tons of people, and on many stages. I got this. We got this. No wait, you've got this God."

I have to admit meeting the other girls who were my competition auditioning for the same role definitely added to an already tense afternoon. Then Psalm 5 came to my mind.

> Let all who take refuge in you be glad; let them sing for joy.
> (Psalm 5:11 NIV)

"Yes," I thought to myself, "Sing, sing for *joy*." Quietly, I sang under my breath, and the anxious thoughts melted away, and peace began to flood my heart and soul. Over the studio loudspeaker, I heard, "Brenda to the stage." "I'm up, this is it!" I had no idea what to expect. I had never done anything like this before. My feet felt like they were filled with lead walking down the stairs to the stage, but all the while, I felt *joy*, unrelenting *joy*. "God thank you for this opportunity, I know you are with me."

Lights, camera, action. The scene began, and my tongue felt glued to the roof of my mouth as sweat began to pour down my back. I felt as though I was dreaming. Then suddenly, when it was time for the first few words to come out of my mouth, everything just seemed to flow, that is until the other actor walked behind me and scooted me to the side because I apparently forgot my blocking, to which I thought, "Oh yeah, I need to move over there." By the grace of God, the scene went well, better than I could have imagined. With a sigh of relief, it was over. I heard "cut," and now the rest was in God's hands.

I hung out at the studio for a short time, walking the halls, hoping this would be a place I would call home one day. Now how to get back home? I called a photographer friend of mine who I frequently shot with. He and his girlfriend picked me up that afternoon from the studio. They were so excited for me that they treated me to dinner that evening. I was exhilarated as adrenaline was still fresh in my veins from the afternoon's events. I never imagined that I would have such an opportunity set before me. Like I've said before, little things do matter so I made sure I paid careful attention to every detail because every little detail matters when preparing for any opportunity.

> Be faithful in the small things because it is in them that your strength lies. (Mother Teresa)

After dinner, I said goodbye to my friends and raced into my apartment so I could call my mom, sister, and friends and let them know how the big day went. I certainly didn't want the evening to end. As the day closed, and the sun went down, I asked God if I could live on this high forever. This was a huge miracle, a huge open door, a big gift from God. I fell asleep with a content heart and spirit lifted as I played the scene in my mind over and over again. Waking up in the morning I was filled with hope and expectation that I would hear from the casting office. Never would I have imagined how quickly. By the time the sun rose on a new day, my phone rang, and it was the casting director saying, "Congratulations, I'm talking to the new Ashley Abbott on *The Young and the Restless*." Immediately, I began to scream with excitement, all the while tears were streaming down my face as the magnitude of the situation sunk into my soul. Once again, I thanked her profusely and said goodbye. Left crying and laughing in the center of my apartment, I got down on my knees and thanked God for this incredible miracle.

What did all this mean? How would this change my life, my future? Could I live up to the standards and expectations not having had any formal acting training? So many unanswered questions raced through my mind but quickly left as I decided to refocus on the fact that I had this new adventure and opportunity ahead.

As you could imagine, my first day of work was daunting and filled with an overwhelming amount to learn. I quickly learned I had a lot to overcome and that I was highly unqualified for this new position, but all the while I knew I had something in me that allowed me to gain this momentum. I knew that something was God. I'll never forget one particular day after being on the show for months now, I finished a scene and the producer came up to me and said, "Uh, you know it might be a good idea to take acting lessons." I was extremely embarrassed, there were actually a lot of unkind things said to me on the set while I was on the show, but this particular comment was a hard one. Once again, I refused to let my emotions get the better of me and resolved that maybe a few acting classes wouldn't hurt. I've always believed that, no matter what, we can better ourselves in life. So, I researched the best acting classes and schools L.A. had to offer and was accepted into a small acting academy off of Sunset boulevard. I enrolled for 6 months. The classes definitely helped me, but I still had much to learn.

While on set one day it hit me: I'm getting paid to learn how to act while employed on this show as a lead character. If landing this job wasn't a miracle from God, then I don't know what was. I remember doing interviews and articles with magazines and newspapers; I would tell them the story of how God opened all the doors, and they would ask me the same question, with a perplexed look on their face, a look I had seen before, "How'd you get here?" I would simply shrug my shoulders and say, "God."

Prayer

Lord, I believe that you have thousands of blessings waiting for me as I trust, obey, and submit to You. That you God will unlock spiritual gifts and blessings in my life that will reap an endless harvest for me and others around me. I agree with Your word that if I "ask it will be given to me; seek and I will find; knock and the door will be opened to me." (Matthew 7:7 NIV)

Challenge Questions

1. Find areas in your life where your sword is dull, your skill is rusty, and sharpen your gifts and talents so you will be better prepared and effective when God opens the door for you.

2. Being young is exciting, but don't allow your youth to become a barrier between you and God, use your time wisely, spend time *with* God which will increase your faith and give you unlimited supernatural open doors. Write two creative ways you can carve out more time with God:

   1.

   2.

11

I was Young and Very Restless

As THE DAYS AND years went on, life began to shift. I became more recognized in public. People started to follow me on the street to stop me for my autograph, take a picture, approach me, and sometimes say the craziest things. Most everyone was very kind and respectful, but I'll never forget one woman who met me and said, "Oh hi, you're Ashley from *The Young and the Restless*, nice to meet you." Then she looked at me up and down and said, "Oh wow, you're much thinner in person. You look bigger on camera." To that, I said, "Uh, thank you?" Another woman asked me for my autograph while I was in the bathroom stall actually going to the bathroom. As politely as I could, I asked her to please wait. This was all very new territory for me. I felt very honored that people acknowledged me in this way.

Then things would really get crazy. I remember being at an autograph signing event at Sears or in Canada, and people would scream my name, and mobs would push their way to get to me. It seemed surreal, like I was in a dream. The strangest thing was people would call me by my character name Ashley. I would say, "Oh yes, I'm Brenda," and they would say, "No, you are Ashley. Look, I even named my daughter Ashley after you." I was naturally honored but confused at the same time.

The fan mail began to pour in, and the assistants would weekly bring bags and bags of mail to my dressing room at CBS. I didn't have the heart to disappoint people so I would sit in between taping and hand sign every photo and send them back to people. I figured if they took the time to write, I can take the time to respond. Settling into my life and character brought even more adventures. As my contract came up, I re-signed for another three years.

During this time, life was moving along well. I was successful, and I was shooting for magazine after magazine cover. My first big nation-wide magazine cover was *TV Guide*, which was a huge honor and a very big surprise to me. That cover brought me other covers, like the cover of *Women's World, Soap Opera Weekly, USA Today*, as well as many European magazines, like *Tele Poche*, and *Tele Jours*. I married a producer, and *People* magazine gave us a six-page spread for our wedding.

Life was moving at an incredible pace. As a lead character on a number one soap opera at the time, I began to receive movie offers and travel opportunities all over the world, which opened a dimension in life for me, but my heart missed my music, so I began to seek out opportunities and jobs that would allow me to use my voice and cultivate myself as a musical artist. I starred in several movies in which I played a character that also sang, which broadened my audience to the realization that I am a singer as well as an actress. I worked with many talented people. I was on a movie soundtrack with Jose Feliciano, Anita Pointer, and the Winans. My husband at the time started directing and producing films. I found myself starring in Lifetime movies, wide released theatrical movies, and working with actors like Randy Quaid, Leah Remini, and Katherine Heigl, among others.

Making these films often took me to the famous, Cannes Film Festival, in the South of France. This beautiful beach paradise was the place to be when you were an actor or actress promoting a large film for the world to see. Every A-list actor was in attendance. The parties and events could only compare to my experience attending the Oscars or the Emmys. The Cannes Film Festival parties were crawling with celebrities, models, singers, musicians, authors, and directors. One evening we were at Hotel Du Cap, and I found myself meeting Mel Gibson, Duran Duran, Gina Davis, Bruce Willis, Jeff Goldblum, and so many others. This was all so fun and exciting, but in the surreal moments, I found myself wanting more and not feeling fulfilled. I wanted to tell everyone about God and share my faith with the people I came across. I wanted to share with them that there is a peace in God that the world cannot buy! As the evening continued on at the packed and extremely famous Hotel Du Cap, the director Renny Harland asked me to sing, and sing I did. I stood on the beautiful balcony overlooking the ocean as the sea breeze wafted through my hair and sang my heart out to a very famous and captive audience. I sang that evening as though I was on the stage of the Oscars. The cool ocean breeze seemed to serve as my background vocals as I sang my heart out and relished every minute of it.

People were blown away, and I was too, quite frankly. I remember thinking to myself, "I always dreamed of being in far-off places, God, but not like this." Floating all of the way home on a beautiful melody, we finally arrived back at our hotel at approximately 5:00 am.

Arriving back in the U.S. with this new experience under my belt put a new spring in my step. The book of Nehemiah talks about leadership. I realized my life affected many others because of the platform God had given to me. I wanted to be a person who others could look up to and a servant who was quick to obey the voice of God. "Keep me humble Lord I pray." Always remember a leader doesn't just lead to gain more followers; a good leader is a person who leads to create the excellence of leadership in others.

> For physical training is of some value, but godliness has value for all things, holding promise for both the present life and the life to come. (1 Timothy 4:8 NIV)

I always made my faith in God known to the people I worked with at CBS. I prayed for various people on the set quietly in other rooms when they shared pains or trials with me, and once while I was an actor on the set with the whole cast of CBS, taking a newscast photo which was to be hung on the CBS walls I once walked with great wonder, I noticed one of the cast members was incredibly upset. I quietly asked if he was okay. He quickly said, "No." He explained to me he may be getting a divorce. With tears welling up in his eyes, he was heartbroken and turning red from the overwhelming grief and sadness. I grabbed his hands pulled him into a nearby room and said, "May I pray for you?" He said, "Yeah, I guess." I prayed a very simple prayer as we had to get back to the photoshoot. I honestly don't remember what I prayed, but I remember my mom always told me to pray for people, and God will use the smallest of prayers in a mighty way.

That moment was a lesson and reminder to me, that the small things we do in faith and love, God uses in such a meaningful and profound way. I felt kind of stupid praying for him because he was the very person on set who used to make fun of me for my faith in front of everyone. He would call me out and say, "Oh, you are that Christian girl, right?" then roll his eyes. People would laugh on set, but I didn't care. I kept a smile on my face and read my Bible on set sometimes. One day in the hair and makeup room I looked at him after yet another snide remark from his mouth about my faith, I pointed my finger at him and with a smile on my face said, "God's gonna capture your heart again one day. You will know him and love him." He looked at me perplexed, didn't say a word, and walked away. It's almost like I was prophesying his future. What I didn't know is that he used to be in seminary, wanted to be a preacher, but then walked away from God.

> As you do not understand the path of the wind, or how the body is formed in a mother's womb, so you cannot understand the work of God, the Maker of all things. (Ecclesiastes 11:5 NIV)

Being married fulfilled my life in a new way, but it wasn't long before I realized I wanted to have a baby. My heart ached for the patter of little feet around our home but finding the time during work and travel became a challenge. I boldly went to the "powers that be" of *The Young and the Restless* and let them know I wanted to have a baby. They made it very clear they weren't going to add the pregnancy to my storyline, but I didn't care. I was heartbroken, but quickly decided I wasn't going to ask permission or wait for them or anyone. I had to live my life on my terms. Approaching almost thirty made me realize that now was the time.

Being pregnant on a national television show isn't easy, I had to hide behind trees, clipboards, sit at desks, and do the floating headshots. My pregnancy was pretty easy, oh except for the fifty-five-pound weight gain. I was huge and it was getting harder and harder to hide my baby bump. Finally, I was at the home stretch almost time to have my beautiful daughter, Sophia, with two and a half weeks to go. I was grabbing some last-minute baby items for Sophia's baby room, when all of the sudden my stomach began to ache. I pulled my car over and grabbed my stomach as the pressure became more severe. I reached for my phone when, abruptly, I felt a rush of warmth down my legs. I looked, and much to my surprise, my feet were covered to my ankles in water. Yikes, my water had broken, now what? I felt okay so I drove home and proceeded to call everyone and tell them we are going to have a baby today. You can imagine my husband's panic as I told him we were having a baby today two and half weeks early while I was driving home. I still needed to pack and to eat one last meal as I knew I had to go on a diet the minute this baby was delivered.

We made it to the hospital but ran into more complications. My daughter was breech in her position and an emergency C-section was in order. I remember lying peacefully in my bed when all of the monitors started screeching and going off. One by one, doctors and nurses started running into my room, and the next thing I knew, I was flying down the hall on a gurney, screaming "What's happening?" Upon waking up, I saw my sister, Deborah, who had flown in with my mother from the east coast. Her first words to me was, "Sophia is fine." I was so relieved; this was not the birthing experience I had hoped for, but as long as my daughter was okay, that was all that mattered. Again I thanked God for my healthy baby as things could have gone very wrong. I knew God had performed yet another miracle for my healthy daughter as I prayed and knew she was marked for destiny.

As the drugs wore off, the pain was so bad from the c-section, I could barely stand up, walk, eat, or breastfeed. Everything seemed so hard and challenging. I wondered if I was going to ever be myself again. Arriving home with my new daughter was a glorious moment until I looked in the mirror and still looked pregnant, so I frantically began trying to lose weight. As I looked in the mirror again, I asked myself, "Who is this person?" I thought once you had a baby most of the weight left with the newborn. Wrong . . . . Much to my dissatisfaction the show called and needed me in a scene on set. I let them know I could barely walk as I had a c-section, but they insisted I come. Not understanding why they couldn't cut my small scene out, I went. Arriving on the set, I was in pain and miserable, popping tons of pain pills to survive the day. As promised, they were careful to get me in and out quickly, which helped.

> They are as sick that surfeit with too much, as they starve with nothing. (William Shakespeare, *The Merchant of Venice*, 1.2)

As time went on balancing motherhood and work became a challenge, the days became increasingly more difficult on the set of *The Young and the Restless*, and at times, the condition on the set was a downright hostile environment. I found myself dreading going to work, and at times, walking through the door of work not knowing who was going to scream at me next. I didn't like going to work anymore and didn't want to rush home anymore as our marriage was in trouble. Something had to give, and I resolved it wasn't going to be me. At work, I was always professional, on time, and knew my lines, but for some reason, I was a target. I was constantly being yelled at over the loudspeaker, told my hair looked like s . . . , my acting was horrible, or ridiculed for some other reason in front of everyone. They didn't yell at others like this, why was I the target? I took it, and I took it, and took it, but one day something clicked in me. When I became a mother, it's as if my daughter Sophia gave me new strength to realize what was important in life, and as a mother, I would never want her to endure this kind of behavior, anger, or malice. I had to decide if this is really what I wanted for the rest of my life. I have always had the mindset: no amount of money is worth your pain or dignity and no matter how much money was thrown at me, "I can't be bought."

Re-signing my contract for the third time would mean financial security, but staying tied to a television contract would never allow me to know professionally what I would be able to accomplish. The show made it very clear that they would not cooperate and allow me to pursue my singing career. They stated they absolutely would not partner with my music endeavors or allow me time off; I had a choice to make, so again, I went to God as I knew there were big decisions ahead.

One day while working on my bags and bags of fan mail, I heard a knock on my dressing room door. It was that same actor I had prayed for. "Come in." He had a look on his face that I had never seen before. I said, "Is everything all right, you okay?" Before he could walk into my dressing room he started to cry and said to me, "Remember when you prayed for me a while back." I said, "Yes." He said, "Something happened. I felt something I had never felt before, and God touched my heart in a new way, and I have renewed my vow of faith and accepted Jesus Christ as my Lord and savior again." I began to cry, we both hugged each other and wept deep happy tears of healing. God has a way of making what is wrong right. When we speak God's word and decree victory over someone's life, death, sorrow, and addictions must flee in Jesus' name. That very simple prayer I prayed in faith, God used to create a firestorm of hope in this person's life. This is a wonderful quote from a strong man of faith Dr. George Washington Carver, an American botanical researcher and prominent scientist, I think his quote fits this scenario.

> When you do the common things in life in an uncommon way,
> you will command the attention of the world.
> (George Washington Carver)

In life, there are going to be triumphs and troubles, but through the power of prayer and the sacrifice of praise we persevere and press on knowing our display of love in action frees and loosens others from bondage. Remember: when God calls you to a task or a position, He will help you accomplish it. When we face opposition, remember: God will fight our battles for us; we need only be still, pray, stand, *Rise Up*, and take authority in Jesus' name.

Prayer

Saturate us in your love, heavenly Father. Help each of us discover your purpose in our lives by laying down our dreams and desires and aligning our hearts with your will and your word. Your perfect plan will unfold every time we say "Yes." Every time we walk away from the wrong, you will lead us into what is right. Tear down idols in our lives that slow us down or cause us to become stagnant, and allow the rich flowing healing waters of your love and peace to overtake us with healing and *joy*.

Challenge Questions

1. What is one thing you can decree over your life today that will loosen the chains of bondage so you can walk in freedom?

2. Prayer is simple. It's as simple as opening your mouth and uttering a few words in faith. Write down a simple prayer you can pray this week that will enlarge your territory.

    1.

3. What are two negative thoughts you can replace with positive thoughts?

    1.

    2.

4. What can you do today to discipline your mind to refocus? Instead, choose focus, choose clarity, choose God. Add one activity that will alleviate stress from your mind, write it down, and follow through.

Perseverance

12

Removing Toxic Thoughts and People

HEAVY FEELINGS OF SADNESS and at times anxiety, made my decision to leave *The Young and the Restless* rather easy. It's important to never allow ourselves to stay subjected to a situation, friendship, or business that causes us constant pain, sadness, stress, anxiety, or fear. Staying in a situation of constant fear or strife brings bondage into our lives. We lose our peace and freedom, and then we begin to lose who we are. We must stop giving our power away to someone who will abuse it. It's so important to be your authentic self and not allow others to squelch your *joy*, creativity, or destiny; after all, an acorn has to leave the mighty oak tree and fall to the ground in order to find a place for itself to plant, take root, and then itself become a mighty oak.

How do you know if you are in bondage? One of the ways I reflect on my life is to check my "*joy* monitor." Are you afraid, anxious, angry, or feeling captive or oppressed by a person, job relationship, or situation? Fear and anger is control, so if you are in a situation where you are constantly afraid or in pain, please take a moment to reflect and ask God to help give you the strength to remove yourself from any toxic or emotionally unhealthy situation, relationship, job, or people, and don't allow another day to be robbed from your life. You are stronger than you know!

> The revelation of God brings the presence of God, and that's when healing begins. (Isik Abla)

Landing another movie role while still on the show boosted my confidence as I simultaneously began heavily pursuing my music career and auditioning for as many roles as I could for film and television. I also began to harness my talents in the recording studio, recording new songs, trying new sounds, and working with multiple producers. In the 80s and into the 90s, it was uncommon to be both a soap opera actress and a recording artist. I was constantly being told "You have to do one thing or the other. You can't do both." I would always ask why, but nobody could ever give me a solid answer. Sadly, I believed it. I really wanted to pursue a recording contract, so I sang at a few nightclubs, which I didn't enjoy, and had some meetings with label heads. They would all tell me I was talented and that they would sign me if I would "change," dye my hair purple, get some tattoos, and pierce my face. I was stunned, unmoved, and resolved that I wouldn't change who I was for Hollywood or anyone. With much persistence and help from my husband, I landed a deal with Sony/TriStar Music. I was ecstatic and elated, but before I signed, I needed to make sure I could fulfill both my television and music contract simultaneously. The music contract required me to travel back and forth to Europe as my producer was located in London, and the soap opera executives made it clear they wouldn't let me off to travel or to record. They stated clearly that they wouldn't support my branching out. In my mind, the decision was made for me as I knew this was another huge open door from God, and I wasn't about to close it. If that meant I had to leave "the mighty oak tree" to become my own seed, so be it; so I left CBS and didn't re-sign my contract with *The Young and the Restless* to pursue my music career.

Signing with Sony/TriStar Music was the most mind-boggling experience of my life. My daughter Sophia was approximately two years old and the love of my life. I spent long hours in the music studio and brought Sophia with me much of the time. The new contract with Sony Music required me to travel abroad to the studio in London to record. I hated leaving my daughter, so I tried to make my trips as quick as possible. I learned so much in the studio and only recorded songs that I felt would inspire others. I often wanted to write some of the songs for my album, but I was told I wasn't a writer and stick to singing. I was so tired of being told what to do, how to dress, how to act, and what I could and couldn't accomplish. I felt pigeonholed, locked in this box, and I so wanted to break free from it. I was exhausted from believing the lie and allowing others to speak limits over me and into my life. I realized, for whatever reason, so many people underestimated me, but once again, just like when I was a child, I remembered God's words over me that my life was meant for more. I held onto that and my faith and terminated my contract with CBS.

Once my album was finished the hard work of promoting the album was in front of us. With the Sony machine behind me, this shouldn't have been a difficult task. Again, God opened another supernatural door. Sony had a great idea to help promote the album mostly in Europe. Why not have me open for one of the acts touring through Europe and place me as the opening act for Lionel Richie, who is known and beloved throughout the world? This was a mind-blowing thought to say the least.

My self-titled album *Brenda Epperson* officially launched in Europe. Rehearsing in sound stages for the upcoming tour was a dream come true. My daughter Sophia was almost three years old at the time, so I brought her with me to travel abroad as the opening act for Lionel Richie. Had I not stepped out in faith from my place of comfort, I never would have known what God had in store for me.

Is there a place of comfort that God is asking you to leave or move from so He can bless you and place you in a new realm just beyond the horizon that is brewing and bubbling up for you? Sometimes we get so comfortable we hide from the possibilities up ahead and become stagnant because change is sometimes scary, we wear a mask of false and fake ideas. We put ourselves in a box which then limits us from breaking out into the unlimited realm. You know, in my own life I had to break out from the false narrative that played in my mind as a young girl: you are ugly, you are fat, you are worthless, you're not pretty enough, you will never amount to anything, God doesn't love you, you will never reach your potential, who do you think you are?

Any of those sound familiar? I actually dated a few guys who told me the same things, they would try to keep me down by telling me I wasn't talented enough, I'd never break into Hollywood, I'm just fooling myself, I'm too old, too young, or you don't measure up. I am here to tell you God did not place you on this earth to exist. You have to break free from those lying voices. There is something very special you have to offer the world and others that is unique and needed right now. I have always shared with others that if there is anything in my life that I have overcome or that inspires you in any way, please know it was by the supernatural power and hand of God. I also have had to get into agreement with the truth of who God says I am. Because the Great I Am is living on the inside of me and YOU.

> If you are tired, keep going if you are hungry, keep going, if you are scared, keep going, if you want to taste freedom, keep going. (Harriet Tubman)

To drown out the negative words spoken over me, daily I would remind myself: I am blessed, I am righteous, I am loved, I am victorious, I am a child of the most-high God, I am an overcomer, I am highly favored, I have the favor of God, I can do all things through Christ who strengthens me, and so can you! You see God opened a supernatural door that the world told me I wasn't qualified for. I walked through it anyway. THAT is the powerful God we serve. I can't wait to hear from you when people start to ask you, "How did *you* get here?"

Before leaving for Europe to open for Lionel Richie, I hired a personal French coach to learn some of the language and culture so I could communicate effectively with the audience from the stage. Using key phrases on stage brought the audience and me to another level of communication and similarities brought us together rather than apart.

Touring with Lionel on the road in Europe was an everlasting memory etched in my heart and mind. I learned so much on the road and performing on stages that Elton John, among others, had just sung. I'll never forget one evening right before I walked out on stage at the famous venue in Paris, France called AccorHotel Arena, which sits on Bercy Street in Paris. This sports arena housed up to almost twenty thousand people, and this one particular evening, it was almost at capacity. I'll never forget some of the people I was with began to visibly shake and feel ill as the crowd began to roar, wanting the show to start. A woman named Susan from behind the stage looked at me and said sheepishly, "Aren't you scared?" I looked at the audience from behind the curtain and looked back at her and said, "No, I was made for this." The moment I walked out on stage, I remember seeing more press people lining the stage than I had seen my entire life. The music began, and with the first note that came from my lips, I felt the music wrap around me which gave me a sense of comfort that overwhelmed me as the vastness of the audience seemed to melt away into the melody of the songs I sang. The roar of the crowd when I finished my five-song set was like a lightning bolt that shot through my veins, feeding my soul with excitement and energy. Backstage Lionel met me with a kiss, hug, and kind words of "You did a great job. You have a fantastic voice." This meant the world to me coming from Lionel. Then he said, "It's showtime," and with that, he made his way toward the entrance of the stage. The crowd erupted in what felt like a huge earthquake, which seemed to feed Lionel's soul as he disappeared onto the stage of the massive twenty-thousand-seat sports arena which had recently housed Elton John and the iconic Tina Turner.

Watching Lionel, Sheila E., and the entire band from behind stage was such a learning experience and a surreal moment for me. I was mesmerized watching Lionel interact with the audience and his talent as he filled the stage with his presence and voice that shook the rafters. As the evening ended a journalist caught up with me and began to shoot questions at me in English like rapid fire. One of the many questions was, "How did it feel this evening performing on the same stage with the iconic Lionel Richie? How did you get here?" There it is again, that same question years later being asked to me again. I looked at him and simply said, "I felt so honored, and it was God. It was all God."

After the concert was over naturally everyone was starving. Ready to eat, I assumed we would do a drive-through for burgers or some wonderful French to go. Much to my surprise and delight, the tour manager announced that we were all going to the famous Paul Bocuse Restaurant Gastronomique, and they were holding the entire restaurant for us after hours just for us. Walking into the restaurant was like nothing I had ever seen before. The opulence and beauty overwhelmed me as I tried to soak in every detail in my mind. The smell of rich French food swirled through the air. The gold candelabras on the table were the largest I had ever seen. The tables looked as though they were set for a king. My mouth had a heart attack once I tasted the fine French cuisine; it was a dining experience that has remained with me to this day.

Every concert, every city, and stage and every audience was different, it was all such an incredible learning experience for me, especially being in a foreign country.

> Every great dream begins with a dreamer. Always remember, you have within you the strength, the patience, and the passion to reach for the stars to change the world. (Harriet Tubman)

The Sony/TriStar machine was well oiled and had me busy with press junkets and interviews, filming in front of the Eiffel Tower, closing the store, and filming inside Christian Dior. I was shuttled around in limos, recognized on the streets, did radio interviews and television shows, and my face was on billboards all across France and Europe. I felt as though I was finally on my way with my music career. After being in Europe for months and the concert tour over, it was finally time to head back to the United States. I know my daughter Sophia was definitely ready to come home.

Arriving home I was met with a very different scenario. Having been gone from the U.S. market for quite some time, when I would interview or audition people asked me where I had been, I explained the exciting events that had occurred, but it seemed to fall of deaf ears. They simply weren't interested. Casting directors would say, "Oh well, that's in Europe. What have you been doing here in the U.S.?" My heart sunk at the realization that I was back to square one with my career.

Watching the radio and record countdown magazines closely, my single "If You Believe," was slowly climbing the music charts in Europe and the U.S., which was great news until an unexpected phone call came through. It was Sony, they called and said the head of the Sony division was fired as well as the entire team that had been working on my album and pushing my single, "A Man Who Talks To Me." They explained that basically every act they oversaw was dropped as well. The cold non-wavering voice said they were "house cleaning." Just like that it was all over. I was devastated. I cried all afternoon, shocked that all of that hard work we just put into the single and the album was over like a beautiful meal that is set before you— once ingested, gone forever. I felt lost and like something very precious had been taken away from me. I couldn't understand how God could have let this happen and how something that seemed so right went so very wrong. "God," I would pray, "I'm trying to use my singing talent for you. God I'm trying to be a blessing to others." God had other plans.

Reinventing myself wasn't easy as I was left to wonder, "Now what?" I held tight to my daughter as I navigated this tough, cold, and many times, cruel world of Hollywood. I plunged myself into church. I began teaching Sunday school and enrolled Sophia in a preschool near our home. My heart was so warmed watching her blossom and meet new friends. She began to flourish, and I tried to use my free time to audition and work on my music. I promised myself I would be a hands-on mother and that I wouldn't drop my kids off at a nanny and leave them for someone else to raise. My family was always first. I never wanted to look back on life and wonder "What if?"

Auditioning in Hollywood proved to be uneventful as the same old roles and the "just take *some* of your clothes off" narrative began to wear on me. That's not who I was, and if I had to take my clothes off to be accepted, then this acting thing wasn't for me. I would no longer allow myself to be under somebody's control or thumb. I was tired of being told what to do or what I wasn't talented enough to do. I wanted to branch out and really explore who I was as a singer and actress. Although trying to find people who celebrated me or my vision proved to be difficult at best. Days, weeks, months, years went by, and I became more disillusioned with Hollywood and the roles that came my way. I passed on more roles than I even auditioned for. I dove into my music which was even more of a difficult task without a large label behind you. As an independent artist (before YouTube), it was almost impossible to get your song on the radio.

My career seemed to be unraveling and so was our marriage. Being from Las Vegas, my husband decided it was time to return to Nevada. I went kicking and screaming but realized this was a last-ditch effort to try to piece back our fragment of a marriage and family back together. I even thought having another baby might help us, but after my miscarriages, I realized the stress was too overwhelming and it was time for me to face the inevitable. We found moments of happiness in Las Vegas, but unfortunately not enough of those moments to keep us together, and our seven-year marriage ended. I learned many things through the divorce. One of the things I learned was I was stronger than even I knew. Once again, I fell on my knees before God and submitted to His will. It was such an incredibly painful time for us all, especially my daughter who was caught in the middle and was a victim of circumstance. Being an only child tossed back and forth was extremely hard on her. I wanted to leave Las Vegas as quickly as possible and get back to work immediately, so I moved back to Los Angeles with my daughter Sophia to focus on my career. God had other plans, plans that would change the course of my life forever.

Prayer

Our sins bring painful repercussions in our lives and the lives of others, but you still love us, God, even while we are sinners. Help us learn from our many mistakes. Help us to be quick to repent and turn from our sins, to be quick to forgive, and to love others as you love us. Keep us humble, mindful, and ever dependent on you. You are our only source of hope and help, Amen.

Challenge Questions

1. How is your faith muscle doing? Are you believing God for a miracle even when you can't see it yet?

2. How can you match your persistence in life with your persistence in prayer?

3. Are you willing to get out of control and submit all of your control to God?

4. Has the control of others stopped you from moving forward in life? How can you remove yourself from a toxic situation, person, mindset, or habit?

5. Are you moving forward in life or are you constantly looking back? God wants to move us into our destiny, but we must get into agreement with Him. Write two promises from the Bible that are for you. Memorize them, hold onto them and speak them aloud every day.

13

Generational Hope

RECENTLY, WE HAVE HAD several deaths in our immediate family; among them was the death of my stepfather who basically raised me. My sister and I had the arduous task of going through four fully loaded storage units filled to the brim with *stuff*. You know, the stuff we accumulate, put in drawers, and then accumulate more. As my sister and I untangled the boxes and boxes of memories, we uncovered some things from our past. We found a Bible from our great-great-great-grandmother, dating back to the late 1800s. While I realize some families have items dating back much further, this was a precious gem for our family. I realized that faith was a strong cord in my family line. I saw a beautiful golden thread of prayer to which my ancestors had prayed, even prayed perhaps for me. As I saw the names written down in the Bible, I realized I am here today because of those in my family line who went before me and prayed for me even before they knew me. My heart burst into thanksgiving over those silent prayers which have held me, kept me safe, and carried me through life's most difficult times. One of the verses I frequently speak aloud from my "Book of Promises" over my family and future generations is:

> My spirit who is on you, and my words that I have put in your mouth will not depart from your mouth, or from the mouths of your children, or from the mouths of their descendants from this time on and forever,' says the Lord. (Isaiah 59:21 NIV)

Make no mistake, our prayers are alive, active, and a secret weapon in the very real battle we face. I believe the prayers we pray out in the atmosphere never die. They stay in the atmosphere and surround our loved ones even after we are gone. When you pray for others, for your family and generations after you, and decree and declare victory, those prayers encamp around your loved ones, hold them, and are used to unlock the potential in your family's life and future generations you are standing for. I am so thankful that my ancestors prayed for me and my sister, mother, and father. Start right now, take a moment to pray for those who are yet to be born in your family line; decree and declare that God will fill them with *joy*, create an atmosphere of hope, revival, change, and strong destiny that this world so desperately needs through your family's heritage. Remember, just as compassion is an action, our prayers are a weapon of change and an action that shifts the future of generations to come.

> Thou shalt decree a thing, and it shall be established unto thee: and the light shall shine upon all thy ways. (Job 22:28 KJV)

Moving back to California with my daughter in the middle of divorce felt like one stumbling block after another. Needing hourly strength, I fell to my knees regularly in prayer. I would seek God in every decision I made. Some days, the only strength I had left was to just sit, read my Bible, and pray. Jobs were scarce, and once again, I was back to square one with my career, having been "gone" for more than two years in Las Vegas. I was out of sight, out of mind.

Where are we going to live? What will I do for work How will I provide for my daughter? These thoughts traveled through my mind daily. Not really wanting to go back into the soap opera world, I did receive a few calls for casting on other soaps which I took for financial gain as my savings was dwindling at a rapid pace. It seemed like all the roles I was approached for had to do with taking my clothes off which I wasn't interested in.

Motherhood is the biggest challenge and most precious gift ever given to me, but raising a daughter on my own as a single mother was incredibly challenging. Sometimes you feel as though you are only as happy as your unhappiest child. Your kids will challenge you and pull you in directions you didn't think you could stretch or bend. Still, I vowed to stay the course and become the best mother I could. I refused to give in to my emotions or looming circumstances ahead. After all, I could only see the immediate brush strokes on the picture; God can see the entire canvas.

Through the miraculous hand of God, a door opened for Sophia and me to move into a brand new condo. While looking at the condo with the builder, who was tall, athletic, kind and he just seemed to have a warmth about him, something miraculous happened. We locked eyes as he said, "Brenda, is that you?" I said, "Terry, Terry Moore?" Just like that, his familiar face melted away all of the stress on my shoulders as the looming weight of my daughter's and my future seemed to lighten. We laughed and shared a few stories from the past, and with one call, Terry said, "You know, I had someone else looking at this condo, but because it's you, it's yours." I was speechless, and I laughed until I cried. Truly, this was another miracle from God.

I have to admit seeing Terry again brought a sense of home to my heart as moving back to Los Angeles felt lonely for sure. God is always at work around us. God invites us all to be in a relationship with Him and to become involved with Him in His work. How do you ask? Faith, it's as simple as faith. Some days faith comes easy and some days we have to fight for our faith, fight even to believe, but when we fellowship with God and in Him, our *joy* is made complete as we are washed in the cleansing work of the blood of Jesus.

Moving day arrived. I would ask Terry if Sophia and I could move some of our things into the condo early, or ask him how to fix the garage, garbage disposal, and on and on. Remember, God not only supplied a home for Sophia and I, but the home was also brand new. Seeing Terry, I have to admit gave me butterflies in my stomach, but I had made a promise to myself: no more men. I was done. I was still in tremendous pain from my failed and painful marriage. I went on to remind myself, "You hate men, remember? You will never give your heart away to anyone again." But even saying those words, I couldn't shake this feeling that began developing for him.

Getting any work proved to be almost impossible. I couldn't even get a meeting with an agent of any kind. I quickly realized I had to become creative. My neighbor had a company and offered me some work at trade shows to help him in sales. I appreciated the work and enjoyed the travels. It's interesting how when everything is taken away from you, you appreciate the small things even more. I used to be shuttled around in limousines and only flew first class; now, I was lucky to get a backseat of an airport shuttle, and sitting in the back of the plane near the familiar stench of the bathroom seemed a constant reminder of how we can have so much one moment, and in another, it can all be taken away. Still, I kept my heart thankful and my nose plugged.

While at the trade show, I met the representative of a company that was looking for more salespeople. They offered flexible hours and work from home, which made it sound like a wonderful opportunity. The home computer age had blossomed. I bought my first computer, set up my email, and created a lovely home office. Working from home gave me the freedom I needed to not miss a single moment with my daughter, Sophia. I never wanted to put her in the back seat. I knew the tender moments of youth only lasted a short time. After all, most likely I wasn't going to have any more children, so I was intentional about squeezing every moment I could with her.

Starting my new job as a "robe associate," a fancy word for robe salesperson, began with a huge bang. I would approach all of the top spas and salons to purchase our robes and embroider their company names for personalization. Most of the time I would mail the robes directly to the spa so I wouldn't have to drive around to each location. This one particular spa was different. They had placed large orders with the company before and since I was the new "robe associate," they wanted to speak to me face to face. I gladly dressed up and I walked into the same spa that I once frequented as a patron. The clean smell of scented candles, freshly prepared cucumber water, and high-end lotions passed through my senses as I quietly wished I was walking in the spa myself for a full treatment. I reminded myself that one day I would be able to afford this luxury again. "Find your *joy*, Brenda, find your *joy*," I kept reminding myself. Hauling all of the robes in my arms was way less glamorous than the life I had previously built for myself, but I was passionate about doing whatever I needed to do so my daughter and I would have a great life together.

Do it with passion, or don't do it at all. (Rosa Nochette Carey)

Sitting in the swanky spa office with my hands full of individually wrapped high-end robes in every color and stitching, I carefully laid them all out for a gorgeous presentation for the head buyer of the salon. I began to make small talk with her when suddenly, she stopped me mid-sentence. She looked at me and said, "Wait, don't I know you?" A bit confused I looked at her and said, "I don't think so." She looked at me intently and said, "No, wait. I know you from somewhere." All of a sudden the realization of where she might know me surged through my body like a lightning bolt; before I could change the subject, she blurted out, "Yes, I know you! You're Ashley from *The Young and the Restless*. What are you doing selling robes?" I died a thousand deaths and sunk into my seat, feeling as small as an ant.

I said, "Yes, uh, that's me." Unenthusiastically, she then looked at me, head tilted, confused, and asked again, "What are you doing selling robes?"

I was really hoping I wouldn't have to humble myself further and actually answer the question, the silence and her deafening stare made me realize that she wasn't going to be satisfied until she got an answer to her question. I took a deep breath and answered the question and with as much confidence and enthusiasm as I could muster. Clearing the dryness out of my throat, I replied, "I'm selling robes so I can take care of my daughter and myself through this difficult time." She had as much compassion as a hungry lion getting ready for the slaughter of its prey. She looked at me, frozen with an inexpressive stare and said nothing, as if that answer wasn't good enough. I tried to break the very awkward silence with a statement, "So I'd really love for you to look at these beautiful robes to order for your spa." Too late, it was such an uncomfortable moment as soon as I spoke, she aggressively pushed the robes off of her desk, shoved them onto my lap spilling all over the floor, and said, "I'll call you if we're interested." Nervously smiling, I said, "Thank you." I couldn't gather the robes fast enough. Leaving the office, my heart sunk. I felt humiliated, not to mention I had just lost a huge account, which meant no money in my pocket, and the realization stung that I was further from my dreams than I had ever been. Eating that humble pie left a very sour taste in my stomach. I cried most of the way home, and I asked God to give me strength.

I was in the battle of my life. My emotions led me down the path of wanting to crawl in a hole and quit while my spirit kept screaming, "Rise up! Rise up! You're meant for more. This is a small step toward your destiny." I couldn't imagine how God could possibly paint a beautiful picture out of such a desert land. I felt dry, alone, and unseen. Would I quit or keep dreaming and trust God to open doors and finances for our future? In tough and challenging times, it's not enough to just know the word of God; we must proclaim it, read it, speak it, decree it, and believe it.

You are made for more. (Lisa Osteen-Comes)[1]

All the while at my new condo my brief encounters with Terry were becoming more frequent as he would come over to help fix various mechanical errors. The more I saw Terry, the more my heart began to skip a beat. He was so incredibly handsome and kind, and his beautiful green eyes seemed to capture and awaken a part of my soul that had died. I'll never

1. Osteen-Comes, *You Are Made for More!*

forget being in my garden in the backyard and my cell phone rang. It was Terry my heart fluttered as I picked up my phone and Terry blurted out almost at the sound of my voice, "You aren't married anymore, are you?" For the first time in a long time, I didn't know what to say, the silence was deafening. I hadn't told Terry anything about my personal life, as I was still healing from the pain of loss and death of my marriage. Terry quickly said to me, "I knew it. I would like to take you out to dinner." Stunned and excited all at the same time I said, "Yes, sure." Wait, I'm breaking my own promise. I told myself I would never trust again, never give my heart away again. When we feel rejected or not accepted by others, we know God always loves and accepts us. God's supernatural, divine love, and the many provisions He has planned for your life, is an unlimited river of resources and cleansing water that is a healing balm transforming us, mentally, physically, financially, and emotionally. God wants to heal us completely, which not only brings glory to His name, but also causes us to rise higher toward our destiny. His complete and perfect love will remove the scars from the past and raise the dead things to a beautiful new life.

Prayer

God give us peace amid chaos, we declare your word out of our mouth. We cut the head of the enemy off and slay darkness, which gives us victory and releases the burden off our shoulders and onto the foot of the cross. Heal our heart so it can move from heavy to light as we meditate on you alone and your word which says, "Come to me all you who are weary and burdened, and I will give you rest. Take my yoke upon you and learn from me, for I am gentle and humble in heart, and you will find rest for your souls. For my yoke is easy and my burden is light" (Matthew 11:28–30 NIV).

Challenge Questions

1. God anoints whom He appoints, He has set you aside to fulfill His purposes in your life, in the life of others, and the world. Ask God to reveal His plan for your life and in the life of others.

2. Say this aloud, I can trust God to guide me, I trust that God has a great plan and future for my life. Read Jeremiah 29:11–14. Write down the things God has already prepared and proclaimed for you and your future.

3. I challenge you today to have the courage to believe God has bigger plans than where you are right now. Will you take a step of courage and believe? Believe that where you are now isn't the end. God has even bigger plans. Write something down that is so big that it scares you, and then believe.

14

Finding Love in the Prayer Closet

OUR LOVE BLOSSOMED AND my trust in men and humanity returned once again. *Joy* was an easy emotion as love and life were taking shape in a way I hadn't known before; this relationship was different than any I had in the past: easy, peaceful, and God was in the center of it. I learned so many things from my first marriage; I learned I was stronger than I had ever known, I learned the things that I could change about myself for my future, and I learned how imperative it is to keep strife out of a relationship and to place God in the center of it. I also learned that anytime I step outside of God's will and follow my own flesh and desires, it never works out. We must trust in God's timing and not push our own timing or agendas in life. I never wanted to step outside of God's will again after all I had been through in my life and divorce. I never again wanted to allow my flesh or emotions to get ahead of God; I realized God has His best for my life and my future if I would just surrender, wait, and trust in Him.

Terry would often tell me I was the "woman of his dreams," and he intended to marry me within a year of our dating. I never imagined I would ever even want to be married again, but with him, it all seemed so easy and too good to be true. He went to a church I once attended and had a beautiful strong faith, which made him very attractive. I explained to him how important it was that we keep God first and pray together; he agreed wholeheartedly. Our true intimacy came as we bonded together in prayer and put God first in our relationship. At times when Terry spoke, I saw the wisdom in him which was such an appealing quality and so important in life. It wasn't long before I quickly fell in love; everything was falling into place so beautifully. I quit my "robe associate" job as the owner of the company at one point refused to pay me my commissions, and I found a job that was better suited for me with a much nicer boss. I didn't want to fight with anyone anymore. Even though my divorce went rather smoothly, I was tired, and I needed a break from all of the strife and fighting.

> The beginning of strife is like letting out water, so quit before the quarrel breaks out. (Proverbs 17:14 ESV)

As the weeks and months blasted forward our dating relationship blossomed into an incredible full-blown deep and very serious relationship. We spent much of our time together. Oftentimes we walked by a jewelry store, and I would comment on the shiny rings, hoping he would ask me to walk in and try one on, but that never happened. As Sophia and I were spending more and more time with Terry, he was talking less and less about marriage, and my heart began to ache. I would drop hints to him about moving to the "next level" in our relationship, and he would say, "What's the rush?" "What's the rush?" I asked myself. We had been together for a year and at this point, all I could remember was at the beginning of our relationship he would constantly say, "Within a year, I'm going to marry you." Now one year later, that conversation had died and so did a piece of me. The realization that this man, who was the love of my life, was no longer engaged in us in that way pierced my heart; all the while God was nudging me to let him go.

Have you ever wanted someone or something so badly that you made it an idol in your life? Perhaps you prioritized a person, material things, or a position above God? God wanted to be my knight in shining armor, not a man. Subsequently, I would sit for hours crying out to God asking Him to change the situation and allow us to stay together, but all the while I would hear in my soul, "Do you trust me?" Of course, I trusted God, but to walk away from the man I truly loved? God must be wrong about this because it made absolutely no sense to me. Days, months, and weeks went by and our relationship became colder; we were approaching a year and I had to consider my daughter above anyone or anything. I refused to "play house." Enjoying dinner together, picnics, and walks on the beach was all so wonderful; almost like we were creating a family, but the reality was, we weren't a family. Terry had been a confirmed bachelor for thirty-eight years, never married and never engaged. I was unguarded and I didn't really take all of that into account when I opened up my heart to him. Terry's father left him and his two sisters early on, and Terry became the man of the house much too young. The painful residual of having an absent father who lived down the street, but who would never spend much time with Terry, or his sisters wreaked havoc on him. Terry genuinely wanted to get married, but a deep-rooted fear caused him to withdraw. As time marched on, being married wasn't at the forefront of Terry's heart.

Finally, the voice of God in my head was so loud, "Do you trust me? You have to let him go." My heart was in pain at the thought of letting him go, yet deep inside I knew God was right. God has a way of convicting us to the point where we are so uncomfortable, we have to do something about it. I even got a call out of the blue from a friend who started the conversation with, "I know this sounds crazy, but I think God wants you to break up with Terry." I cried, "You've got to be kidding me." More tears flowed as sadly; this conversation confirmed everything.

One night while Sophia was sleeping, Terry and I were sitting on the couch watching television and, talking. I took a deep breath, and I heard that same voice again in my spirit again asking, "Do you trust me?" I whispered, "Yes, Lord." I gulped, looked at Terry, and I said, "Where do you see our relationship by the end of the year?" He looked at me blankly and became agitated, and said, "I don't know, why do we need to talk about that?" Those words were like a knife into my heart. Shocked, and realizing I had my answer, I looked at him calmly and I said, "If you don't know that you want to marry me after a year, then you need to leave." With that, he looked at me, didn't say a word, and started to walk out. I chased after him and said, "Say something?" He told me he was scared. He'd been a bachelor all of his life, and he didn't know if he could take all of this on. All of this on? To which I told him, "How sad that your fear is greater than our love." The door slammed behind him. Was it over? I was surprisingly calm and definitely in shock.

Days and weeks moved ahead, and I told Terry we needed to take thirty days to clear our heads, we shouldn't see each other or talk, we needed to take time to pray and think, and after thirty days, if he wanted us to "move forward" in our relationship, he would call me; we both agreed. I felt confident that after a year of dating, he would want to move forward and get married. I prayed prayers like, "God, please make him want me as his wife," or "God let him only have eyes for me." You guessed it. Thirty days rolled on and no call. I was broken; how could this be God? I did what you asked of me God. I was even obedient. You told me to trust you, and I did, now look: my heart is more broken than ever. We were even staying pure in the relationship.

I would cry out night after night in my "prayer closet." I cried guttural, bitter tears, angry at times and pleading to God saying, "This obedience thing is stupid: it doesn't work. I've done everything you've asked, God, and you still took him away. How can you say you love me and want the best for me, God, and take away the man whom I love deeply, the man who awoke something in me that was dead. He's perfect God, why?"

> In your anger do not sin: do not let the sun go down on your anger. (Ephesians 4:26 NIV)

If you have never heard of the term "prayer closet," it is actually mentioned in the Bible: Matthew 6:6 says, "But when you pray, go into your room (or closet), close the door and pray to your Father, who is unseen. Then your Father, who sees what is done in secret, will reward you" (NIV). I had always heard the term "prayer closet," but I had never tried it before. I was desperate, so that's exactly what I did; I locked my closet door behind me, and day after day, I cried out to God for help. I was angry. I felt betrayed by Terry, I was scared, and I was confused and unsure about my judge of character. Mad at myself, and frustrated with God, I exclaimed, "This obedience thing doesn't work God. I did what you asked me to do, and he still left."

Something beautiful happened in that "prayer closet," something that has enhanced my life, and to this day, I am better off from that pain I endured and the trust that was etched deep into my soul. I died in that closet. Everything I longed for died. Everything I thought would fulfill me I laid down at the cross, and my future was a blank canvas. I fully submitted to God. I simply pictured myself falling back into the arms of God, eyes shut as I said over and over and over again, "I trust you, Lord. I trust you, Lord." Some people call it a "war room," but whatever you call it, find a place in your home you can shut the world's distractions out, quiet your spirit, and commune with God; maybe even bring a pen and paper and write down the words or strategies God unveils to your heart and mind.

Sometimes, like it or not, God will give us an exercise in overcoming the flesh. Feeding the flesh causes it to grow even larger; denying the flesh shuts it down until our flesh dies. Denying the flesh deactivates it, then the flesh along with those unhealthy desires slowly lose control over us. We are no longer held captive; we are freed from bondage.

Our culture elevates the wealthy, but God elevates the humble. Our culture elevates the world's way of doing things; God says His ways are above our ways and His thoughts above our thoughts. Following the world's desires will never satisfy us. Worldly ways are an insatiable desire to want more which brings about greed and gluttony, which then deludes our minds, causes confusion, and convinces us even when we have so much, we need more, and we will never be truly satisfied or fulfilled until we get it. That's a lie. God says, "Follow me and I will give you *joy* everlasting and the fulfillment of the desires of your hearts." He is our fulfillment, when we give God everything we have and all that we are, He will, in turn, give us everything He is.

I had always been a fan of Joyce Meyer. In fact, I found her in the infancy of her ministry, and her words soaked a healing balm into my heart. I even wrote to her personally during my divorce and sent her an offering with a prayer request, and she personally wrote back and thanked me. Her words were profound: as she explained, when God brings someone or something back, He brings it back better than it ever was before, or He moves us into a new direction and a better place. My heart still ached for Terry, but he was nowhere to be found. Finding my *joy* in those days was often difficult. I clung to my Bible, and I began to memorize scriptures and speak them aloud. I began to decree and declare God's promises into my situation which brought an incredible and profound strength to my soul. It was in those quiet moments in my "prayer closet" that the rebirth of memorizing scripture began; every day I would repeat and memorize as many scriptures as my brain could hold. It was as though when I spoke the word of God into my situation, God's word would annihilate the enemy's stronghold over my life and the pain associated with certain circumstances. Even though my heart ached for Terry, there was a rebirth beginning in my spirit. I was starting to *Rise Up* on the inside with a new understanding of God's power and in the nuggets of spiritual gold found in His word that I had never known or understood before. I switched gears and poured into my daughter Sophia: I became the Girl Scout troop leader, the class monitor, and the after-school parking lot volunteer. Work was hard to find, but God would always send me jobs that supplied everything we needed. All the while His gentle whispers of, "Do you trust me?" would blow through my ears.

Waiting in the carpool at school one day my phone began to ring with an unmarked number. In my spirit, I knew it was Terry. Stubborn as I am,

I didn't answer. Months had gone by, and to me, our relationship was over. Besides, if he wanted me, he knew where to find me. I pressed harder into God, and Terry's messages on my machine started piling up. In his messages, he never said the words I needed to hear: "I want to spend the rest of my life with you." He would only call to say, "Hi, just checking in," as though we were at some casual place in our relationship. It took everything in me not to call him back, but I'm pretty stubborn, and I resolved I only wanted God's best for my life and my daughter's life. I would never ever again settle in anything in my life; I never wanted to step ahead of God again. God began to heal me as I humbled myself, and when I asked for forgiveness for making my relationship an idol, an incredible healing began to flow into my heart and soul.

I arrived home one day almost three months to the day Terry and I had parted ways, and there were two dozen beautiful roses at my door with a note. I cried as I read Terry's words, but yet again, nothing was indicating he had any intention of spending our life together. I couldn't go back to "playing house" as my daughter's heart was also on the line; she was so hurt when he disappeared.

Back in my "prayer closet," I shared my deepest most intimate heart's cry to God. I poured out my anguish as my love for this man was still so deep. With bitter tears, I wept, "God, I love this man so deeply." I held Terry's nine-page letter in my hands, reminding God: "I walked away. I let him go like you asked, but if you don't want me to have him, if he's not your absolute best for me in my life, then I surrender. I trust you, God. I will walk away and fall back into your arms blindly." My flesh was dying, falling off in big chunks as well as all of the small hard pieces. The hard barnacles on my heart became softer; I was more submitted and less rebellious. I finally moved out of the way, so God could supernaturally work on my behalf, so HE would get all the glory, honor, and praise for the glorious things He has done. I know He wants to do the same for you in your life as you submit and surrender.

> I have been driven many times upon my knees by the overwhelm-
> ing conviction that I had nowhere else to go. My own wisdom and
> that of all about me seemed insufficient for that day.
> (Abraham Lincoln)

Being freed from the weight of all of that unforgiveness and heaviness I didn't know I was carrying, loosed me into freedom. I began to forgive myself, the boy who raped me when I was six years old, people who spoke evil things over me at different jobs, those who tried to control me, past friendships, betrayal, my family, my ex-husband, and Terry. The damaged root of my flesh was being plucked out, the dead, dark places became healed, and I was released into freedom from years of anger, bitterness, and hard-heartedness.

My heart still ached for our relationship, especially after reading Terry's contrite letter. A friend of mine told me to call him back, thank him for the flowers, and explain to him that he should move on with his life and that I am doing the same. Why I took her advice I have no idea. That's exactly what I did. I left a message on his home machine while he was at work, and I told him I was moving on with my life and thanked him for the roses. I ended my call with, "Please tell your family, hello, and I miss them." I had grown so fond of his family.

Weeks later while at home with Sophia I heard a knock at my door, which was unusual as we had gates, and nobody could get to my door without ringing the buzzer. I looked over my balcony from the second floor, and I called out, "Who is it?" Much to my surprise, Terry popped out. His eyes were bloodshot, and he had lost a significant amount of weight. I was astonished; my heart was pounding. I slammed the window, and I ran to Sophia who was all of nine years old, watching cartoons. I shouted, "He's here, he's here. Terry is here, what do I do?" She looked up at me and she said, "Mom, open the door." I replied, "Right, I'll open the door." I ran downstairs and I nervously opened the door. As soon as I saw Terry's face it was simply a natural reaction to hug him. We embraced and we both broke down and cried. The next thing I knew, Terry was down on one knee, placing the most beautiful engagement ring I had ever seen on my hand—true story. He asked me to marry him right then and there. Of course, I said yes. God is in the business of healing and restoring; no *thing* and no one is out of His reach.

God has a way of making the crooked places straight. God brought Terry back better, surer of what he wanted, and without any doubts or reservations. I had to be fully convinced that God was able to do what he promised. I needed to get in agreement with His word and align with His will. Terry and I were both restored individually and then God brought us back together better and made all things new.

Prayer

Dear Lord give us the strength we need to walk away from possessions or people that have become an idol in our lives. The Bible says that, with God, all things are possible. Help us believe your word and hide it in our hearts. Give us confidence in your power and in your strength. Heal me according to your will. Let your life-giving power rest on me, reside in me, and flow through me. Restore everything that is dead and bring it back to life. Wash me whiter than snow. In Jesus' name.

Challenge Questions

1. What are you going to lay down today? What do you need to repent and walk away from?

2. What is something in your flesh that needs to die? Once you lay it down, leave it to God, leave it at the foot of the cross, and put one foot in front of the other towards your complete freedom in Christ.

3. Has the valley of your tears turned into a dirty mud pit? Ask God to release the fear, anguish, and pain from your heart, so you can *Rise Up* in *joy* and move forward in clarity and peace.

4. "Rejoice always, pray without ceasing" (1 Thessalonians 5:16–17 ESV). Memorize it!

5. All throughout the Bible, when people or a nation were in trouble, seeking change and help, they would fast. Traditionally, fasting is a denial of food, submitting yourself to prayer so you can focus on God. I want to challenge you today to open your mind to another type of fast: fast from gossip, negativity, anxiety, and fear. Fasting is a spiritual secret weapon if you will. This discipline yields a surplus of benefits, not only in our lives but in the world. What is one or more emotions you can fast from, for a day, a week, or a lifetime?

15

My "Book of Promises"

GOD'S TREMENDOUS LOVE FOR each one of us comforts us, knowing while we were still in rebellion and sin, He gave His life for us. I am constantly reminded of this living proof of His love.

Life was moving at a fast pace. Excitedly, Terry and I decided in the next six months we would tie the knot in Hawaii with a small group of dear friends and family. Hawaii (the island of Lanai) was the first big trip Terry and I took together while dating. We loved the Hawaiian culture, beautiful rolling beaches, the calm, healing, medicinal waters of the islands, and the "aloha" essence of love and peace that Hawaii brought to our soul. There is an old Hawaiian prayer called Ho'oponopono which talks about love and forgiveness and making things right in your relationships. All of this tropical beauty resonated in both of our hearts and seemed to call us back to these incredible islands.

The planning and preparation for the wedding was absolutely *joyful*; Terry's sister's husband, my soon-to-be brother-in-law, is a minister so he married us in the only Christian church on the mountains in the small community of Lanai. It was a dream wedding; the chapel, painted perfectly white, seated only about sixty people and was nestled between beautiful Hawaiian Cook Island pines. You could almost feel the history and love wrap around you the moment you entered this quaint chapel. My precious sister Deborah was by my side the whole time along with my parents.

It felt like a dream walking down the aisle in my big white formal wedding dress with my beaming father and my precious daughter, Sophia, as the flower girl, wearing a white lace dress and a handmade flower wreath on her head. Locking eyes with Terry, I saw a tear run down his cheek; it was priceless. I'll never forget my father crying as he gave me to Terry or the look on Sophia's nine-year-old face and the audible gasp of our guests when Terry bent down during the ceremony to give Sophia a ring. He stated, "I'm marrying you too, Sophia. This is a promise to you as well." Her face blushed as Terry put the ring on her finger. I began to cry, almost to the point where I couldn't stop.

Now it was time for the vows and "I do's." Terry shared his vows with me and when it came time for me to speak, there was complete silence. All of a sudden I had this overwhelming feeling when I caught a glimpse of my precious mother-in-law and sisters-in-laws, all the kids, and my family out of the corner of my eye. I was overcome with the fact that God had truly ordained this. This was God's perfect will for our lives. I could see my future, and God's purpose and plans were unfolding. It's as if time stopped. I could hardly breathe, and I started to cry as the "prayer closet" memories came flooding back into my heart. I heard those precious words again in my spirit standing before God and everyone at the little altar of that Hawaiian church. "Do you trust me, Brenda?" To which I quickly said in my spirit, "Yes, Lord." I literally couldn't speak. My brother-in-law finally cracked, "Well, maybe she's having second thoughts!" Which broke the awkward silence. Finally, I was able to say, 'I do." There wasn't a dry eye left in the little white chapel on that beautiful Hawaiian afternoon.

> Therefore, since we are surrounded by a great cloud of witnesses to the life of faith, let us strip off every weight that slows us down, especially the sin that so easily trips us up. And let us run with endurance the race God has set before us. We do this by keeping our eyes on Jesus, the champion who initiates and perfects our faith. Because of the joy awaiting him he endured the cross, disregarding it's shame. Now he is seated in the place of honor beside God's throne. (Hebrews 12:1–2 NIV)

We decided to start a family quickly, which was an enormous change for us all. Sophia was the tender age of nine, and the school she attended wasn't her favorite; all of the change and, at times, chaos, took a toll on her heart, for sure. I tried to be there for her in the deepest way that I could, but I was preoccupied and regretfully at times not able to be there for her as much as I should have. On the weekends she would leave the house to go to see her father which would rip my heart out. I would cry half the evening after watching her leave; I always dreaded Fridays and the time Sophia and I spent apart.

Settling into our new lives together proved to be challenging at times, especially for my husband who had been a longtime bachelor, playing weekend sports for much of his life. Being a husband and an instant father was a huge transition for him too. Thankfully, he was up for the job. Although, when a huge truck filled with all of our stuff arrived at his home on move-in day, the glassy look in his eyes and terror on his face said it all. "We're here!" I said. He looked, waved us on and walked into the house, and then he came back out and said with a stunned look on his face, "Where are we going to put everything?" When there's a will, there's a way!

It wasn't long after our new marriage that I quickly became pregnant. The excitement of a new member of the family was palpable. I hadn't told Sophia about the pregnancy due to my last miscarriage, but telling Terry that he would be a father for the first time was a moment I will never forget. I sat down and handed him a gift bag. As he opened it and he pulled out the tiny pink baby shoes, the look on his face was priceless; he said nothing at first, then when the realization hit, I saw a little fear mixed with *joy* whirling around in his mind; we hugged and laughed and were both elated. I must have conceived on our honeymoon as we were still newly married. There was so much hopefulness in our lives, like a doe running to fresh grass. I was twenty-nine when I had Sophia and being ten years older with this pregnancy, deep fatigue set in fast during the first few months. I was so lucky that I never got nauseous. Actually, I had the opposite problem; once I conceived, I was like Jabba the Hutt. I couldn't stop eating! Most of my days were spent unpacking boxes, eating, and trying to blend three different lives together, which was tons of work.

Waking up one beautiful weekend morning I felt a little strange. Almost three months into the pregnancy, I arose from the bed and I felt wet. I looked down and the bed was filled with blood. I panicked. I immediately called Terry in tears, barely able to speak. I mumbled, "Meet me at the doctor's office. I'm bleeding." Shaking and praying all the way there, I felt numb and fear began to grip my heart. I fervently prayed, "I need you God right now. Heal me please. Help my baby." I don't remember getting to the office, the parking lot, or even walking into the doctor's office. All I remember was being in the room with the doctor with my husband standing next to me and the doctor looking at us shaking his head saying, "It was twins, they're gone. I'm sorry." "Noooooooo!" I yelled as the tears poured from my eyes. My heart dropped and the devastated look on my husband's face was enough to make me want to disappear. The disappointment on his face broke me. I felt like a failure. I felt like I missed something and the fear of not being able to have another child became real.

We had a meeting with the doctor a few months later and he told us to go ahead and try again, that it was probably a fluke and these things happen. Getting pregnant again felt like a miracle. I shared the news with Terry. He was so happy, but I could tell he was cautiously optimistic. Keeping my hope and eyes fixed on God I resolved to remain steady and determined that this time all will be well.

A stunning moment occurred when I was driving in my car and blood began to pour. I was about ten weeks pregnant this time, still in my first trimester. I raced to the doctor's office. My nervous husband met me there and the same words came from the doctor's mouth: "There's no heartbeat," and this time he added, "You can't go home. You have to go to the hospital right now for a DNC. You have an infection. We have to do this now or you could be in physical trouble." "What?" I replied, completely shocked. "I have to get Sophia from school." Looking at the doctor squarely into his eyes, I said angrily, "No, I'm not going to the hospital. You can't make me." Calmly, he looked at me and then at my husband, and he said, "I'll leave you two alone for a few moments." Clearly, he had experienced the unpredictability of a hormonal, emotional, pregnant woman before. "This can't be happening again," I said, crying uncontrollably to Terry. The sadness etched on his face was more than I could bear. Gently he said, "You have to go or you'll get sick." As hot tears of deep agony fell down my cheeks, I just kept saying to him, "I'm sorry, I'm sorry, I'm so sorry." I felt like such a disappointment.

Staying overnight in the hospital felt like weeks. It felt like a dead-end, and a deep sadness slept in my hospital bed that night. When I arrived home, I locked the bedroom door, crawled into my bathtub, and sobbed. I opened my eyes and watched the bathtub begin to fill with blood, which was a constant reminder of what I wanted so badly, but I couldn't have. Without realizing it, I placed Terry and our relationship as an idol in my life. I realized I was doing the same thing with wanting to have a child so desperately! I was placing my entire self-worth, our relationship, and my identity on whether or not this child would be born. Despondent, weak, and weary, I looked at all the blood around me in the bathtub and I wanted to panic, but instead, something more profound happened. A feeling of transcendence rose up in me. I heard that familiar whisper from the Lord in my ear in the bathtub at that tender moment, "Do you trust me Brenda?" In deep prayer and hot flowing tears, I said, "Yes, Lord I trust you." I then began to sing and worship and thank God and speak aloud through my bitter tears in that blood-filled bathtub, "I trust you, God. I trust you, God."

Those were hard words to utter as my circumstances did not align with anything good or promising. My emotions certainly did not necessarily align with those words coming from my mouth, but my spirit bore witness to what I was confessing out of my mouth, according to God's word, which caused my faith to grow. I knew God would somehow work good in this situation. As I spoke those words out of my mouth, from that blood-filled bathtub, my heart, soul, and spirit began to strengthen. Below is a beautiful prayer of confession, there IS LIFE and power in the word of God. I decided to stand constantly on Roman 8:28, "God works together all things for good" (BSB).

> Surely the arm of the Lord is not too short to save, nor his ear too dull to hear. (Isaiah 59:1 NIV)

Hearing the news from our pediatrician that there was nothing else he could do for me to try to get pregnant again and that he had to refer me to a specialist, was humbling, to say the least. This took a toll on me, my daughter, and our marriage. Instead of bringing Terry and I closer, I felt a distance, but I refused to give up. *Joy* was slipping out the door. I decided to get aggressive with God's word. I would wake up before Sophia went to school, and I memorized scriptures like, "She is clothed with strength and dignity, and she laughs without fear of the future" (Proverbs 31:25 NLT). I wrote scriptures on my hands and arms, and I began to speak scriptures into my future before I saw any of it happening. In faith, I was calling things into being that were not as though they were, in accordance with Romans 4:17. When I was in my car, I posted scriptures on sticky notes, and I did not allow a moment of fear or doubt to take root into my thoughts.

> If you fully obey the Lord your God and carefully follow all his command, I give you today the Lord your God will set you high above all the nations on earth ... The Lord will grant you abundant prosperity-in the fruit of your womb, the fruit of your womb will be blessed. (Deuteronomy 28:1, 11 NIV)

My belief was definitely challenged when I met with the specialist as she went down the list of everything that might be wrong with me and my womb. I began the long series of blood work, scans, dyes shot inside of me, and small evasive, painful female surgeries. Still, they found nothing. I wasn't sure if that was a good thing or a bad thing. After months of testing, all of the holes and bruises on my arm made me look like a drug addict. The specialist looked at me and said, "I can't find anything wrong, so try again. Take some progesterone and estrogen and let's see what happens." Getting pregnant wasn't necessarily the problem; keeping the pregnancy was the struggle. I thankfully conceived again, rather quickly, and I felt encouraged when I saw the slightest line on the pregnancy test I held in my hand. I knelt on the floor and I whispered, "I trust you, Lord." I called the specialist and she said, "Get in here now." Racing to her office, they took blood and prescribed progesterone and bed rest. Days melted into weeks, weeks into almost three months. This was the longest I had ever kept a pregnancy, other than Sophia. The day came that my husband and I went to see if there was a heartbeat. My mind went back to the bathtub and the scriptures I declared over my womb out of Deuteronomy 28. Lying on the table felt like an eternity with sweaty palms and a racing heart, but I resolved that no matter what, I would not be moved, and I would completely surrender and trust God.

> In God I trust and am not afraid. What can man do to me?
> (Psalm 56:11 NIV)

The baby's heartbeat sounded like a locomotive racing through the doctor's office. There it was, life beating strong, a new life growing inside of me. My husband and I grabbed each other, and we just sobbed. This time they were happy tears.

God's faithfulness was proved over and over again. Upon our baby girl's birth, soon after another baby girl arrived. Life took a new blissful turn as our young family was growing. With three radiant girls, our hearts were full of deep gratitude for all God had done for us. Sophia finally got the siblings she had always wanted, and I was able to give Terry two more beautiful baby girls, which caused our marriage to grow more deeply.

Birthing two kids back-to-back, I realized I was a little behind on my doctor check-ups. I made my appointment to have my routine mammogram. The only thing different about this appointment was after my screening the doctor asked me to wait in a separate room which was a bit unusual, although I didn't think much about it at the time. All of the sudden, the door opened. I'll never forget it was almost as if everything was in slow motion and a heaviness walked in the room with the doctor. She looked up at me from the file and said, "I have some news for you. Upon looking at your mammogram findings, you have breast cancer." I froze. She then turned and said, "I'll be right back." I sat there in this dimly lit room trying to process what was just said to me, still frozen in the same position. Looking at the closed door, I felt that heaviness creep toward me. Before I knew it, I felt something creeping toward my legs. Unfreezing my neck I consciously looked at my feet as though I would see something. I saw nothing, but I felt something start to creep up from my toes, and I realized it was moving up my legs toward my knees. I began to lose movement in my feet and my legs were beginning to go numb, that heaviness and fear was trying to paralyze me.

Something started to *Rise Up* on the inside of me. It was the Holy Spirit, and I spoke aloud in that doctor's office a scripture I taught my daughter: I whispered aloud, "I will not fear I will trust in God; I will not fear I will trust in God." Over and over again as I was speaking that scripture out of my mouth looking at my legs. That same gripping, numbing, dark terrifying spirit that was crawling up my legs trying to choke the life out of me and paralyze me in fear, stopped and began to reverse its course and head back down my legs, this time in the opposite direction, and I was free! That my dear brothers and sisters is POWER. That is the power of God and His word! Make no mistake when you speak God's word out of your mouth you will see the manifestation of it either immediately or over time, but God's word never returns void. That's a promise; that's His promise to us.

God in all of His love protected me, and the diagnosis was caught early in the beginning stages of cancer. I saw so many doctors I couldn't keep count. I had needle biopsies and surgery to see if possibly they would be able to remove some of the cancer. While I was in the radiology room, I looked around at the patients that were in critical stages in their precious life. The smell of sickness and death was palpable; under my breath, I said, "I refuse this. This is not my future. This is not your best for me God." I looked at each person in the face, and in my heart, said a prayer for their lives.

I was moved into another room, and while waiting to speak to the doctor about the next steps, there was a knock on the door, and a woman came in. She looked very serious and said, "Hello." Immediately, I looked up at her and smiled the biggest smile I could and said, "Hi, how are you?" I could see she was visibly shaken. She looked directly at me and said, "Are you all right?" Confused, I looked back at her and said, "Yes, I'm great how are you?" She said, "I can't believe you're smiling. Most people are having such a hard time." I looked at her directly and said, "Well I choose *joy*, and

I am trusting God to heal me." I learned so much from my past trials and triumphs. God was my firm foundation this time, and I would fight back the devil in prayer and faith. She smiled looking relieved and said, "Well, I'm from the department of mental health, and I came here to help you but looks like you helped me. I'm even smiling again." Isn't that incredible!?

God moved me swiftly through cancer as it was caught in the early stages. There was no radiation or chemo needed, just a few surgeries and a new level of faith. He is sovereign.

> You will keep in perfect peace those whose minds are steadfast, because they trust in you. (Isaiah 26:3 NIV)

I continued to write life scriptures in my "Book of Promises." Quoting these scriptures aloud almost every day breathed new strength into my spirit. This was my way of chronicling all the miraculous things God had done for me because we tend to forget the blessings when we are in a time of prosperity and rest. I often refer back to those breakthrough moments in my "Book of Promises" when life throws me a curveball, and looking back on those scriptures encourages me and reminds me of God's great faithfulness.

Prayer

Say this prayer and scripture out loud: "Those who trust in the Lord are like Mount Zion which cannot be shaken but endures forever. As the mountains surround Jerusalem, so the Lord surrounds his people both now and forevermore" (Psalm 125:1–2 NIV). Lord let us be a people who are consistent in our prayer and faith. Let us not be shaken by the changing world. The scepter of the wicked will not remain over us as long as we remain and abide in you. Anoint our lips with grace, not hate, and may your mercy and goodness always triumph over evil. We will believe, we will stand, we will *Rise Up*, we will trust and never surrender and remain completely unmoved. In Jesus name.

Challenge Questions

1. What are some things you are grateful for? What are some things you are longing for? How can you trust God today in a deeper way?

2. What are some things you have given up hope on? Invite God into that hopelessness.

3. What distractions can you remove from your life to free up your time with God?

4. What are some things you have grieved over, but are still causing discomfort and brokenness in your heart because you haven't laid them down and trusted God?

5. Humility comes when we allow God to transform our hearts. Write down one or two places you need to ask for forgiveness and become more humble.

6. Almost every morning I wake up and say, "I'm desperate for you, God." Say these words and watch Him transform your attitude, heart, and your day.

7. We cannot let our emotions get the better of us. What is one emotion that has tried to control you that you can walk away from: anger, easily offended, gossiping, critical spirit, unhappiness, negativity, or perhaps impatience? Now, strategically walk away from those emotions and don't let another day be stolen from your life.

16

Pulling the Weeds

"SHE TOOK MY TOY! Stop hitting me! Mom, tell her to get out of my room!" Sound familiar? I love the *joy*ful boisterous sounds of our children that bellow through the hallway of our home. Trying to raise happy successful children in conjunction with building a strong marriage is like balancing an open bag of tiny pebbles on your head while walking across sheets of broken glass. Sound difficult? Well, it is! A life verse that I cling to and repeat often is one that helps me in critical times of much-needed balance in my life.

> Unless the Lord builds the house, the builders labor in vain.
> (Psalm 127:1 NIV)

Don't despair, help is on the way! Don't throw your hands up and lay down just yet. God wants us to work in partnership with all He is doing. God is not against human effort, but working alone without adding God into the equation causes our labor to be in vain, and the fruit in our lives isn't often as abundant as it could be. We must remember: even though at times our children can be "*joy* killers" when they are fighting and arguing with one another, they are also God's greatest gift, an inheritance from the Lord. They are our greatest asset, not a liability. He trusts us with these young innocent lives to shape and mold, and hopefully, our imprint will continue for future generations to impact the world.

> Start children off on the way they should go, and even when they are older they will not turn from it. (Proverbs 22:6 NIV)

One day while I was loading my young kids into their car seats, I turned on the air conditioning to cool the stifling summer heat. One of my favorite songs came on the car radio, "Amazing Grace." I turned it up really loud with all of the car doors open while I snapped the buckles on my children's car seats. Peace and serenity rang through my heart as I sang the soothing lyrics: "Amazing Grace, how sweet the sound that saved a wretch like me. I once was lost, but now I'm found." One of my daughters suddenly threw a hard object at the other which set off a firestorm of wails that echoed through the car into the busy street and pierced my eardrum. While the song "Amazing Grace" was blaring from my car radio my kids were shrieking, crying, and hitting one another. I screeched, "Knock it off, quit screaming, stop yelling! I'm sick and tired of you guys fighting. Now stoooooooop!" My kids froze as the bellows of my screams echoed through the truck and into the busy street. Painfully aware I was being watched, I looked around at the concerned pedestrians who stopped dead in their tracks with hostile stares. They frowned and shook their heads in disgust at this crazy woman screaming at her children with Christian music blasting in the background. I sheepishly looked around, sighed, and thought "Well, with one fell swoop I have just completely ruined my witness to anyone." That's not true! We are all human and we all lose our peace at times. Thank God His mercies are new every morning!

Being a mother of three is so rewarding and also incredibly challenging. I took a long hard look at my life. Yes, I had to let some things go. I had to prioritize and put some things on hold to raise my children.

You can have it all, just not at the same time. (Maria Shriver)

My personal sacrifices were tough, and at times, another lesson of my flesh dying. I'm not the best at always following the rules. Sadly, my pride and ego have to constantly be chipped away. Early on in our marriage, I remember when my husband Terry was leaving town and he asked me not to drive his brand-new exotic car with the high-performance engine. Immediately, I inwardly became indignant and I thought, "I'll show him! When he's gone I'll drive it anyway. He'll never know!" Death to our flesh never comes easy, and Terry might have never found out if I took his new car for a spin, but God knows. He is omnipotent. I fought with God back and forth so many times, and every time I walked to Terry's fancy new car to drive it, I heard this in my mind "Deny the lesser to gain the greater." With a deep sigh and a half-willing heart, I relented, and I prayed, "Yes, Lord."

I began to learn the true meaning of selflessness; I didn't always have to be in first place. Sometimes the highest sacrifice we can make is when we put others first, not in an imbalanced way of losing who we are, but to raise children who are world changers, we need to pour our unconditional love into their lives. I also had to take a long hard look at the people I had placed in my inner circle. I wanted to grow; I wanted to fulfill the calling on my life. To do so, I had to weed my own overgrown muddy garden. Have you ever noticed that when you plant a seedling of any kind, the growth of the plant depends on the soil it's rooted in? I had some beautiful "vines" in my life that were not growing so well, so I had to clear the weeds (people) around that were perhaps slowing me down or delaying my destiny. On the surface, I couldn't see what was happening, but underneath there were problem roots that still needed tending and pruning. I pulled the weeds and added some fertilizer to give my "vines" the richness they needed to bear fruit. It's not that the vine isn't growing; the plant's growth was being stunted by the weeds around it and not able to bear fruit.

A weed is but an unloved flower. (Ella Wheeler Wilcox)

Parenting is much like pulling weeds. Every day we not only need to be refreshed in His word, like a well-watered garden, but we also need to water our children with prayer, grace, forgiveness, hope, respect, boundaries, and unconditional love, because the weeds in our children's lives will stunt their growth and not allow them to perhaps reach their full potential. It's the exact same way in our own lives. We need to take a look at who and what we are surrounding ourselves with and what we are allowing to enter into our hearts and minds. When you give yourself away it usually doesn't happen all at once. It's slow, gradual, and it's usually the small everyday compromises that slowly chip away at our heart and soul. We must stand firm, stay awake, live courageously, be kind, and be on guard against all of the enemy's schemes in life.

It is the image of God reflected in you that so enrages hell; it is this
at which the demons hurl their mightiest weapons.
(William Grunall)

I'll never forget sitting with an acquaintance I hadn't seen for a while who had starred in some very prominent A-list movies. With tears in her eyes, she revealed how she gave so much of herself away, having sex with so many men, compromising her beliefs to get a role or the next big part in Hollywood. She went on to say something that struck me so hard,

"Brenda, all those pieces of myself I gave away, I can never get them back."
My heart broke for her as I tried to share that God's love will not only
renew her life, heart, and mind, but He will also make the crooked places
straight and the rough places smooth and wash her white as snow. God
can take all the pieces we gave away and replace them with His everlasting
treasures. Take a moment right now to make a conscious decision that
you will no longer compromise what you know to be right, and resolve
that you'll make a commitment to remove toxic people and things that
may be stunting your growth.

Prayer

Gracious heavenly Father, in all of your infinite wisdom, open our eyes
and our heart in this season. Reset our soul, so we can see what is holding
us captive. Let us never compromise, so we are not exposed to the risk or
danger of lowering our morals or standards. Release our minds into the
supernatural realm of healing and the sacrifice of praise.

Challenge Questions

1. What are some weeds in your life? Maybe it's a relationship or a job. Identify what needs to be pulled from your heart and life and write it down.

2. What impact have I made in this world? What impact have I yet to make in this world?

3. Heaven and hell are both seeking agreement for your identity, which will you say yes to? How will you pivot in the battle of the mind to reprioritize? Remember it starts small.

Chapter 17

Help, There's a Teenager in My House

MAKING TIME TO HAVE fun with our children will bring *joy* into all of our lives. My daughters and I would sometimes turn the music up really really loud all over the house and dance our brains out, laugh, and en*joy* one another. I have learned the art of not taking it personally when my kids look at me with complete disgust on their faces when my dance moves are so "old school" to them. I laugh and say, "Well, I'm having fun!" Choose to focus on the *joys* of parenthood, try to recall why you took on this important role, and approach parenting with thanksgiving in your heart. Having one daughter already out of my house, I can tell you every time I walk by her room, I miss her. For all of you single moms out there, I have so much respect for you, and I want you to know that I think God has reserved a special place in heaven just for you to rest and put your tired feet up in a mansion that is the biggest on the block with a 24-hour cleaning service.

Observing the hard work it took for my mother to raise the two of us all by herself, I underestimated all of the hard work and sacrifice it took. She made it look easy. God calls us to serve our children. I must admit that is not always something I'm good at! My old body of sin wants to be served and much of the time I want my own way, which does not work very well when you and your child are both having temper tantrums. All too often we become complacent in our position of parenting and our children, husband, and family suffer for it. The word "permanent" simply means everlasting or a longtime function; that is a word that I believe God wants us to use while parenting. Make a decision to *Rise Up* and become a selfless parent for your children permanently, for as long as we all live.

Holding my peace and trying not to overreact during the teenage years has been a Herculean effort. I am teaching my kids to guard their hearts, which at times has proven to be an enormous undertaking. One of the parenting strategies that I use with my children is friendship. While I am definitely their mother, they understand that my word is my word. I also think one of the most important strategies in parenting is to be able to keep your eyes open, your knee pads on, and an open line of communication with your children. Make it fun for your kids to come tell you things they would otherwise tell their friends. If they say, "Oh! I wanna tell you something" stop and drop everything and give them your undivided attention with excitement. Let them know you are really interested, which shows them that you care. Learn to control your tongue when you want to freak out, and just listen.

> Do not be anxious about anything, but in every situation, by prayer and petition, with thanksgiving, present your requests to God. And the peace of God, which transcends all understanding, will guard your hearts and your minds Christ Jesus.
> (Philippians 4:6–7 NIV)

As parents, oftentimes we are so concerned about laying down the law or meeting our own schedule we forget to develop trust with our child. A teenager or child will only talk if we have worked on laying a bed of trust for them to sit on. Even when sometimes they are reluctant. What's involved in the bed of trust? Remembering to not overreact, for example: while sitting with one of my daughters having an evening conversation, she all of a sudden opened up to me. She said very casually, "Remember when I went with my friend a few months ago to a movie?" I evenly replied, "Yes." She continued, "Well, we didn't go to the movies when you dropped us off at the theatre. Her friend picked us up with his friend, and we went over to their house." My body went numb. My tongue was on fire as I choked back my fury and anguish. The fear welling up inside of me was like salt on an open wound. Trying not to scream from the pain of what would come out of her mouth next, I swallowed deep. I whispered in my spirit, "God help me," and calmly asked her, "Oh? What did you do there?" Bracing myself for her answer, praying God would give me strength, she admitted, "It was really awkward as my friend went into the room with the one guy and shut the bedroom door. The other guy and I just sat in the living room on the couch, and we looked at each other. It was really uncomfortable." My heart stopped as my palms dripped sweat. I followed up with, "What did you guys do?" She said, "Nothing. He was really nice, we just sat and talked and waited for them to be done. Then they dropped us back at the theatre in time for you to pick us up." Choking back the fury wanting to come from my lips, all the while in my mind saying, "Hold your peace, Brenda. Hold your peace!" I finally muttered "Well, I appreciate your being honest with me." I wanted to throttle my daughter for allowing herself to be put in such a compromised situation! I try to use these "teachable moments" for my children with a little cup of guilt, which can be effective too. I told her, "Thank you for telling me this. I appreciate your trusting me with this conversation, but you know you could have been raped. You know that behavior is completely against what I have taught you. You lied to me. I know you are way smarter than that. I know you have better judgment. It's extremely important who you hang out with. Were you scared? Do you realize that something horrible could have happened to you? The thought of that breaks my heart. I couldn't live with myself if something happened to you. My heart would have broken in a million pieces." I reminded her that God was watching over her. I have always tried to live by my actions, as my words mean nothing if my actions don't align. She confessed, "I know, Mom. I know." I was scared and I prayed the whole time while I was sitting on the couch. I hugged her and we both cried, holding tightly to one another. I told her how thankful I was that she was okay. Help me, Lord. Get the knee pads out! See, if I had overreacted, yelled, accused her, our line of communication would have been severed. After all, the situation was already done and over. This was not a common problem we faced; it was a one-time circumstance. The worst position we can have in our kid's life is the position of them being afraid of us. Fear never provokes conversation; fear intimidates, shuts others off, and closes doors of trust.

In grade school when my daughter was having a major struggle with a teacher who was inappropriate in the way she spoke to my daughter, I set up a meeting with the teacher to discuss the issue. Do you know what she said? "Your daughter told you what happened?" I countered, "Yes." "Wow, I never told my mother anything," the teacher revealed. "I didn't trust her. I can't believe you guys have that kind of relationship and your daughter shares her heart with you." As the teacher's eyes welled with tears, something melted off of her that day and we never had another problem. Wow, what a great lesson. We need to eliminate and resist the need to conquer and break our children. What they need is the unconditional love of Jesus shown through your actions and words, your heart and ear, along with a healthy dose of accountability, discipline, and rules.

I'm not perfect by any stretch of the imagination, nor am I an expert or authority on parenting, but my three girls have taught me a few things. When at times they or I become out of control, trying to get our point across, I really try to be the one to stop the strife immediately. I then get my anointing oil out; I anoint the pillows, bed, doors, bathroom, and closet chairs, and I write scriptures on small pieces of paper and place them in my kid's pillowcases and under their mattress. I refuse to give way to strife and arguing. By placing the word of God on the bed in which they sleep, I believe they are circled, not by the enemy, but by God and His word. It's like giving your kids medicine for their souls. Don't be naive; we have an enemy that wants to take our families out, destroy our hearts, kill our relationships, and wreck our homes. You and I must stand firm against these attacks by being the bigger person, knowing our authority in prayer, and leading the way into peace and strife out of our homes.

He must become greater, I must become less. (John 3:30 NIV)

Once my toddlers were growing and getting older, finding the right Bible study was a lifeline for me. I found strength with a few women who were "global-minded." What I mean by that is they were constantly constructing prayers and thinking beyond what they could see. This excited me and ignited a new flame in my spirit. I kept hearing from various women in the prayer group, "You are called to the nations, Brenda. You know that, don't you?' Overwhelmed and bearing witness in my spirit I could barely utter "Yes, I know." Once I said those words out of my own mouth it was like a firestorm started on the inside of me, and once I spoke it aloud, I immediately got in agreement with who God had called me to be. I was in agreement with my identity. If there is one thing I know for sure: if Satan can steal or rob you of your identity, then you will fall for any entrapment or lie that is set before you. Satan cannot steal your destiny, but he can cause you to give it away. Dear ones, never allow the world or the enticing lies of darkness to steal your identity and the perfection that resides on the inside of you. What God has placed on the inside of you is exactly what is needed right now to heal the world.

This new firestorm in my soul opened my mind to infinite possibilities of what God could possibly do through me. I began dreaming big dreams again, remembering when I was a little girl at camp, the miracles I saw and personally experienced, realizing that those far-off lands I envisioned as a young girl weren't so far away anymore. I carried that with me in my soul all those years. I began hearing God's voice, His small whisper in my soul more clearly and louder.

One day while sitting by the pool minding my own business, I heard God's so clearly in my right ear saying, "I want you to start a women's conference." "What?" I thought. He said the same thing to me three times, I was stunned and confused, because if you handed me a blank piece of paper and asked me to write my wildest dreams on it or something I wanted to accomplish while living, never in a million years would I have written a women's conference. I kept this tucked in my heart, but while praying at the women's Bible study, I was overwhelmed with emotion as my spirit stirred. While in tears, I blurted out, "God is calling me to start a women's conference. I have no idea what I'm doing. I have no idea how to do this. I'm scared. I don't know what to do." Sobbing I broke down in tears as they all gathered around me and prayed. I kept saying it's too big. I've never done anything like this before. I forgot about the fact that God is bigger.

> If the dream you have doesn't scare you, it's too small.
> (Mark Batterson)

Months went by, and I was now leading my own Bible study, which I never imagined. When the pastor's wife (who led the study) was moving, I told the women that I was sad that the Bible study was ending. They all looked at me and said, "What do you mean?" To which I said, "What do *you* mean?" They looked right at me and said, "You are going to lead us." Never imagining myself in that position I quickly said, "No I'm not." Just as quickly, they all said, "Yes you are." There you have it, another moment in time in which I never imagined would happen.

I started sharing with the women about what God whispered in my ear about starting a women's conference and asking them if they wanted to help with anything. I began to make calls to my church asking about rooms and dates, still having no idea what I was doing, all the while pressing harder into God. While watering my garden, I heard God's gentle whisper and voice again in my right ear, now almost six months later after telling me He wanted me to do this conference, but this time, He said three things to me. He said, "Women will be saved, set free, and my name glorified." I almost dropped the hose at the realization of the almighty trusting me with this daunting vision. Suddenly, it began to take shape in my heart and mind.

One day while praying I heard the name of someone I had known for awhile pop in my head. God, once again, whispered in my ear to call her. I felt like I was losing my mind, but I picked up the phone, called her, told her the story about what God whispered in my ear, and then out of obedience, asked her if she would like to be a part of this movement God placed before me. Before I could get the words out of my mouth, she excitedly screeched "YES!"

As Ascend Women was born, now in our ninth year, we have seen the mandate fulfilled. Women's lives have been completely transformed and renewed by the power of God. Women have been delivered from depression, fibromyalgia, and addictions, and truly His name has been glorified.

I shudder to think what would have happened if I had said no to God even though I was too afraid to move forward. Sometimes you have to just do it afraid and let the God of the universe fill in the blanks. Obedience requires adjustment. You cannot stay where you are and grow with God at the same time.

Prayer

We declare peace according to your word: "Peace I leave with you; my peace I give you. I do not give to you as the world gives. Do not let your hearts be troubled and do not be afraid" (John 14:27 NIV). When we are overwhelmed with pain or sorrow, we will overwhelm our problems with your word. Thank you for healing us through the power of the Holy Spirit. Anoint our lips with thanksgiving, and remove the deep pain of loss from our souls. Restore us to health, and heal our wounds. In Jesus' name.

Challenge Questions

1. Let's take an exercise in overcoming the flesh. Decide to fast something; give up anything that is not bearing fruit in your life. Being uncomfortable activates personal development and improvement that leads us toward growth and peace, instead of grief and strife. What can you overcome today?

2. What are some things you can do to prevent problems that are caused by pride?

3. He knows you by name. Do you know His name? Write down five names for Jesus. What do they mean?

4. What is one thing that you can learn from in your past so you don't repeat it?

Chapter 18

Staying Plugged In

EVEN NOW WRITING THIS I have tears in my eyes as I am saying goodbye to my dear sister who spent part of her summer with us and is now leaving back to the east coast. Like my sister, I also had to say goodbye to a dear horse I took care of named Henry. I felt so lucky to be the guardian of him for a short period of time to help out a friend. Probably sounds crazy to some, but I get so attached to these animals it's so hard to say goodbye. Have you ever heard that saying?

> Work like you don't need the money. Love like you've ever been hurt. Dance like nobody's watching. (Leroy Satchel Paige)

It's tough to wrap our minds around giving ourselves emotionally or physically to someone, not knowing if we will receive that love in return. Animals are a bit different. They love you no matter what you look like, sound like, smell like; no matter your background or financial status. It's a type of unconditional love that most of us humans never receive or give, sometimes in our whole lives. I have always been passionate about animals because of their unconditional love, among many other beautiful qualities. I also love the fact that animals don't talk back, but unfortunately, they don't stay in our lives forever either.

When we are truly able to walk away and turn from the hurt and pain that was caused by someone else, or that we inflicted on ourselves because of our own poor choices, that's when we become freer to love as we've never been hurt, and that same freedom allows us to open ourselves up to forgiveness. True forgiveness and repentance allows us to turn from anger and bitterness and move forward freely which then causes us to be filled with more *joy* as we let go of our past and move toward our bright future and the over three thousand promises in the Bible that God has for each one of us. It is only then that we are freer to, "Love as we've never been hurt."

How do we keep our *joy* if we are so afraid and scared of facing or dealing with pain? What you are chasing after may one day chase after you, so make sure you are moving forward focused on the right things with a Christ-minded focus. If we refuse to deal with pain-causing issues, we tend to close off or lash out at others, rather than face the truth about ourselves or someone else.

> You hypocrite, first take the plank out of your own eye, and then you see clearly to remove the speck from your brother's eye.
> (Matthew 7:5 NIV)

How do we react in kindness and compassion to others if we carry the bondage and chains of the past pains with us everywhere, we go? At some point, the bondage is all we see, all we feel, and all we know. It wraps its way around our heart, mind, soul, and body. It's all we project when others look at us.

Being kind, compassionate, and full of faith helps us stay plugged in to God, others, and the world. We need to be mindful and continue to give freely to others, while expecting nothing in return, to people we know, people we don't know, people who deserve it, and people who don't. For me, staying plugged in means taking time almost every morning to read scripture from my Bible, recite a scripture out loud, meditate on God's word and goodness, and pray. This helps take the focus off of me and plug into the great I AM; after all, none of us are perfect, right? None of us are really deserving of the supernatural kindness and grace that is ours freely. What makes us deserving? We deserve to be loved because of what Jesus Christ did on the cross for us. When we "love like we've never been hurt," we stay plugged into His grace, which I believe also gives us *joy*. Too many of us are walking around lifeless, unplugged, and disconnected from people and life. Some of us are afraid to say hello, or just not even wanting to be bothered. We have forgotten how the small, seemingly insignificant things in life *do* make a huge difference and positively manifest themselves. Not only in our lives but in the lives of others. We need to always remember to take the time to step out of our own hurt and worries, make a decision to unplug from worry, fear, anxiety, physical struggles, and strife, and plug into God, others, the planet, and what's happening around us. Actively throughout your day, look for someone, anyone you can bless and help. Sometimes we remain so focused on our own life's problems or hurried schedules that we don't notice anyone else. That's a huge problem, a huge imbalance, and causes us to become disconnected and stagnant.

I was at a large international airport recently—tons of people full of hustle and bustle; so crowded you were almost running into people as you walked down the hallways to get to your own gate. I found myself looking down just trying to get another twenty gates to reach my destination, when all of a sudden, I felt a nudge from God as if he was saying, "Look up, notice the people around you." So, I did. I really try to not be on my cell phone when I'm walking around, that way I can purposely notice people. I don't always accomplish this task, but at least I'm trying. Suddenly, almost immediately, once I looked around at the people passing by, I noticed a young boy walking slowly down the hall. He was walking toward me but over to my right side, wandering and looking around, and as he came closer towards me, I noticed the panicked look on his face. I myself was racing to my gate as they were calling all passengers on board. As he passed by me I thought, "Oh, he's okay." Then I took one last look back, and the boy just stood there and stopped. I thought, "Oh no, this little one is lost." I turned around and said, "Excuse me, sweetie, are you okay?" He looked at me with his little lip shaking and said, "No, I'm lost." Then this precious six-to-seven-year-old boy just burst into tears. I said "Okay, okay, sweetie, it's going to be all right. I'll help you. Let's walk over to this gate. What's your name?" He said, "Jonathan." I quickly grabbed an airport personnel who "happened" to be walking by. I told her the story as we walked to my gate.

We walked Jonathan back behind the ticketing counter, and I asked the flight agent if they could intercom through the airport to help find his parents. I began to ask Jonathan some questions to help ease his mind and quiet his little tears. I wanted to pick him up and hug him tight, but I knew having this strange lady hold him would probably be inappropriate and scare him, but my heart just ached with every tear that fell from his beautiful eyes. Upon asking Jonathan where he was going, he said he was from Vietnam, and he and his family were on the way to Utah, bless his heart. As the ticket agent began to page Jonathan's parents, people in line started looking at him and me. They would ask, "What's wrong? What happened?" I began to tell them he's lost. People would gasp and say, "Oh no, that's terrible," or "How'd you find him?" I explained to them what happened.

By this time, I'm starting to get nervous as his family hadn't come to claim him, and the ticket agent said to me, "Ma'am you have to get on your plane. The flight will be leaving soon." Determined to make sure Jonathan was okay, I would say once again, "Just one more minute." Finally, when I couldn't wait any longer, I slowly made my way to the plane hallway. I turned to assure Jonathan he was going to be okay and his family would arrive soon. Just then, as soon as I turned around for the final time, I saw his family running over to the counter. The relief on all of their faces made me smile and filled my heart with so much *joy*. Our eyes connected with a smile, we waved, and he disappeared in his family's arms as I walked down the corridor to board the plane.

My heart was so *joy*ful and thankful that I was able to help this young boy, but something else began to happen while I was sitting in my seat. As I finally made it to my seat and the line of people skirted by me, I began to hear people talk about the situation as they passed by. One girl said, "Did you see what happened out there? That nice woman helped that boy. He was lost and that nice lady helped him find his family." Then she said, "Wow I guess there are still people out there who are good and help others." While sitting in my seat another person walking down the aisle of the plane said, "It gives me hope that there is still good in this world." I was stunned when I came to the realization that something I did had a ripple effect on people's lives. I had no idea the people watching this unfold would be touched and affected. The people looking on were given hope.

When we look up, out, and *into* the eyes of those around us, we will notice life happening, we will become plugged in and aware of people's needs, and actually become a part of our world, a part of our surroundings, and begin to feel a part of the pulse and the heartbeat of life, rather than walking around feeling alone and isolated. When we bravely "love like we have never been hurt," the love and *joy* vibrations are astounding. Remember, nothing is too small. Lady Gaga recently stated in an interview, "The fantastic thing about kindness, is that it's free, and it brings us all together."

> Joyful are people of integrity who follow the instructions of the Lord. Joyful are those who obey His laws and search for Him with all of their hearts. They do not compromise evil, and they walk only in His paths . . . As I learn your righteous regulations, I will thank you by living as I should. I will obey your decrees. Please don't give up on me! (Psalm 119:1–3, 7 NIV)

I just wept when I read this verse as King David poured out his heart. It's so challenging to stay away from evil, to not compromise, and to not judge others all at the same time. We as a people should long for righteousness, walk in truth, run from evil, confess our faults, repent, and walk in humble obedience to God. I don't know about you, but one of my prayers is "God don't give up on me, and don't let me give up on you."

That word obedience, or obey, really always freaked me out! In my life many times, in many ways, people have abused their authority over me, which caused me tremendous pain and distrust, and as a result, caused me to rebel, a lot! Rebellion doesn't work so well in a friendship, marriage, school, work situation, or any relationship for that matter. Rebellion grieves the Holy Spirit and separates us from God's promises and plans for our lives. Rebellion is an open door for Satan to enter, attack and eat away at our conscious. Honestly, I have always been a bit of a rebel, but I have learned, if we are going to rebel against something, let's rebel against what the world says is okay, and plug into God's word and what HE says about our lives and those around us. We find rest and peace when we trust, believe, stand, and have faith in HIM; that is where we find our power, authority, peace, and the fullness of *joy*! When we are living in the fullness of our destiny it is an overflow that spills into and touches the lives of everyone we meet in our local area and then vibrates around the world.

> "A creature revolting against a creator is revolting against the source of his own powers–including even his power to revolt. It is like the scent of a flower trying to destroy the flower." (C. S. Lewis)

The world tells us: just stay focused on earning more money, more cosmetic surgery, buy the latest hand-bag, clothes, take a vacation, buy a bigger car or home in order to be filled with happiness and *joy*; but those things are temporary; the newness doesn't last, it wears off and what we once thought filled us fades away. We need to stop looking to ourselves, to others, or the world, all of which are limited. We would be substantially more fulfilled if we looked to the ONE who created us and asked Him to fill us with *joy* and remove the empty dark places with HIS light because HE is the light of the world. God's word explains to us that salvation is a free gift. You don't have to do anything, just receive. He did it all and paid it all when He sent His son Jesus to free you, heal you, forgive you, and FILL you with *joy*. All we need to do is ask.

If I could leave you with a few things to think about today it would be: never stop praying, being kind, doing what's right; never stop doing little things for others; never stop believing that your life can and will be full and filled with "*Joy* unspeakable and full of glory." *IJOY. We are all in this together.*

Prayer

Unleash your wisdom in our hearts and in our lives. As we humble ourselves before you, raise us up from lies, anger, and rebellion into peace, love, and tranquility. Let us not waste one more day drowning in defeat or unbelief. We cast our cares on you because we know you care so much for us.

Challenge Questions

1. What's one thing you can unplug from today that is causing you anxiety, worry, or frustration.

2. What can you plug into that will give you peace and feed your heart, your mind, body, soul, and spirit?

3. Have you experienced such deep gratitude that it almost felt natural to thank God? If not, what is one thing you can be thankful for today?

4. What's one lie that you can unplug and walk away from and exchange it for and plug into the truth?

5. What is one tangible step that you can take to be around more people that lift your spirit and are full of HIS *joy*?

6. What do you need to unplug from and plug into that will bring you more daily *joy*?

19

Racing against Time

DO YOU EVER FEEL like you are racing, running against time? This was never more true than in November 2018. I awoke from a deep sleep to the sound of my phone ringing at 3:00 am. It was my oldest daughter, Sophia, on the other end, crying. I sat up and said, "What's wrong, honey?" She said that there'd been a mass shooting at Borderline. "I'm afraid some of my friends might have been there." I began to pray with her and reassure her, but she couldn't shake the feeling of pain and sorrow that seemed to loom over her that morning in the newsroom where she worked.

Several hours later, I finally fell back asleep—just before my alarm went off to get my other daughters up for school. I still felt a heaviness in my heart and spirit as I turned the news on and began to see the horrific pictures and images of that evening's mass shooting at a place called Borderline, not far from our home. I prayed all morning, but my spirit still grieved and my heart was still hurting even as I drove my kids to school. I prayed with them, kissed them goodbye, and felt an overwhelming urge to drive straight to the site where the shooting took place. I knew in my spirit I was to go there and pray fervently.

Not knowing where I was going, I relied on my navigation, which took me in circles. I pulled over, prayed, and asked God if perhaps he didn't want me to go further, or maybe I should turn back, but I felt a *GO* in my heart and spirit, so I forged ahead. Within minutes I began to see emergency trucks and vehicles lining the streets, which indicated to me I was finally going in the right direction. While getting closer, my heart and spirit sank as the evil and darkness became so palpable. I parked my car as close as I could to all the road-blocks and police tape, then began walking toward the shooting site, praying with each step and claiming the land back to God.

> Arise, walk through the land in the length of it and in the breadth of it; for I will give it unto thee. (Genesis 13:17 NIV)

I knew what I was supposed to do. Right there on the curb, I knelt down and curled into a ball on my knees, face down while praying and crying out to God. Approximately an hour later, I heard a voice saying, "Excuse me, are you all right?" I looked up, wiping away my tears, and saw a man standing next to me with a camera under his arms. He said, "I am a Christian, can I pray with you? Are you all right?" Welcoming this moment, I said, "Yes." He knelt down beside me, and we began to pray. This stranger said many things as he prayed, but then he said something while praying that struck my spirit. He said, "You have wisdom, a voice, and people need to hear what you have to say, so speak." I was stunned. Little did he know this was something I have battled with over the years. My thoughts turned to what I could say that would possibly help anyone. Why would someone want to hear what I have to say? I took what he said into my heart and silently said a prayer of agreement over his words. What made it easier is that this wasn't about me at all, and his words struck a note within my spirit. I then prayed for him and continued my prayers for everyone affected by this senseless Borderline tragedy. Then the stranger I had briefly met left. At times, I often wondered if he was, perhaps, an angel sent to speak words I needed to hear. I felt a bit more peaceful in my spirit as I buried my head back into the ground and while on my knees, I prayed for a while longer. Once I felt the heaviness in my spirit leave, I stood up and began to leave the scene. By then I was stunned at the number of news trucks and camera crews that had arrived. I felt it was definitely time to go. The one scripture that kept running through my mind and my spirit was: "If my people who are called by My name will humble themselves, and pray seek my face, and turn from their wicked ways, then will I hear from heaven, forgive their sin and heal their land" (2 Chronicles 7:14 NKJV).

Upon heading home I drove past a friend; we waved to each other, then she and I called each other. She informed me that her friend had three friends die in the Borderline shooting. Her sadness was significant. Instinctively I made a U-turn and met her for coffee so that we could talk. My prayer was that I could be of some support to her during this very dark time. I tried to comfort her the best I could, and we spent over an hour together during which time I managed to squeeze a laugh or so into the conversation. Looking at the clock, we both left for our homes.

Although I felt better, I still couldn't shake this aching heaviness in my heart and spirit—a different kind from the heaviness I experienced at the Borderline site. I continued to pray in the knowledge that so many people desperately needed to be lifted up in prayer that dark day.

I left our home to pick up my kids from school, and as I was approaching the school building, I was stunned to see gigantic plumes of smoke from what looked like a fire in the neighboring mountains. Californians are majorly aware of the telltale signs of a wildfire, and this was a sight I had learned to dread. As I picked up one of my daughters (the other had after-school practice), I tried to keep up the semblance of a regular day by going to our favorite deli to pick up dinner, but there was something ominously different about this day. As we departed from the deli, my daughter and I saw the ever-thickening black smoke up the street, and we both looked at each other concerned, saying, "Is that the same fire or a different one?" We quickly realized there was a second fire headed toward us from the opposite direction. Within this short November 8th day, it felt like there were calamitous forces piling up one after the other. My heart was still heavy. We raced back to the school to grab my youngest daughter from practice early, as I explained to the coach I was a bit worried about the fires, not to mention the air was now thick with smoke. We jumped in the car as my oldest daughter called me again worried. I shared with her my concern about what looked like two severe fires headed towards our home and town.

Increasingly aware of how badly this day was unfolding, I called my husband to find out his whereabouts. At that stage, I was anxious to have my husband with us as soon as possible, but Los Angeles is an uncooperative city when it comes to traffic congestion, and he was stuck in the middle of one of L.A.'s worst traffic jams. With the worsening situation, it was really important to me that I had my family all together under one roof (with the exception of my oldest daughter who lives out of town). As my husband's car eventually came into our driveway, I breathed a massive sigh of relief—not knowing that the relief would be short-lived as the momentum of what was about to be one of California's worst days in history unfolded. Within twenty minutes I received an anxious call from a friend who lived approximately fifteen minutes away. She told me that their family had just received fire evacuation orders from the county sheriff. My immediate response was to ask about all the animals she kept on her property. I knew she didn't have a trailer and as a family we jumped into action, offering our trailer so that we could rescue their mini-farm animals—all forty of them! We ended up taking two trucks and a trailer, and as we drove in, I saw that she was visibly shaken and genuinely frightened. What accentuated the reality of the unfolding horror was the live television coverage that showed the burning destruction of homes, animals, and the land, as the evil forces of the fire swallowed everything in its path. The fire was now dangerously close to her home. The increasingly ferocious flames demolished everything in their path. Land, homes, trees, people, and animals. This was a massive wildfire like nothing we'd ever seen. It was unrelenting and unstoppable.

Together the two families prayed as we gathered bunnies, turtles, horses, goats, and a few necessary provisions. Time, however, took on a new dimension. Just as we had rounded up our friends and animals in peril, all of the sudden, we heard the phones light up which sounded like screaming. The evacuation orders had escalated to an emergency "go now." Time had run out. The fire was dangerously close. It was leave now or die!

With hearts pounding, we raced away with forty-eight animals in the cars and trailer, heading back to my home and farm, for what we hoped would be our safe sanctuary. The taste of embers on our tongues, however, gave us a sickening sense of foreboding.

The kids had fun placing the goats in the stalls while the chickens and all the other animals had a special place of safety in their new temporary home. As God would have it, I had put just enough food in the oven before we ran out the door. I heated the food and had the exact amount to feed two families. Isn't God good? He thinks of everything. We ate, the kids played, and we continued to watch the news, as the fires seemed to gain speed and cover more ground, area, and territory. But even as we watched the nightmare unfold on television, we convinced ourselves that there was no way the fire would come all the way over to where our home was. We kept a close eye as the kids grew tired and fell asleep. My friend and I hopped in the car and drove around to make sure there were no flames in the nearby distance. Not seeing any flames we felt somewhat comfortable, we all decided at about midnight to go try to get some sleep.

My phone rang at approximately 2:30 am. As I grabbed it, I heard my other friend hysterically saying, "We have to evacuate! The fire is here. It's here. Can we come to you? We have to leave now. I am scared." I saw my husband fly out of bed; he ran downstairs to check outside while I ran out to our balcony. What made this so frightening is that my friend lived only ten minutes away from us on the other side of the freeway. I opened the balcony doors and couldn't believe what I saw. The air was dark with the ash-laden smoke creating an eerie silence that was the quietest, loudest sound I had ever heard. I was stunned as I listened to the sounds coming from our large pasture where there were approximately thirty horses that our neighbor had evacuated near our creek. There simply weren't enough trailers to haul them out. You could hear the horses whinnying and kicking. Obviously, they were all very, very agitated. I began coughing as I breathed in the thick smoky air. I called my mom on the east coast, woke her up, and said, "Mom, pray in agreement with me now." For some reason, I felt as though it was important to have a person agree with me in a prayer of agreement according to Matthew 18, "Where two or more are gathered in HIS name." I said, "Mom, I think we have to evacuate." Our sense of safety at home was cruelly short-lived.

The atmosphere that night will linger in my memory forever. It was a strong sense of pervasive evil in the air; an eerie presence not unlike what I had experienced at the Borderline site that very morning. My mom and I prayed fiercely as I stood on my balcony with my arm raised to heaven. I began to speak in the language God gave me, to the mountain near our home and claiming protection and scripture over our home, neighbors, animals, and everything we owned. Psalm 91 began to pour from my mouth as my mother and I prayed in agreement. We hung up as soon as the fire angrily gobbled up the precious commodity—time. I woke everyone in our house as we desperately called around to find more trailers in anticipation of our mandatory evacuation. My stomach sank as I realized that our trailer could only hold three horses, which wouldn't even be large enough to evacuate all of our own animals. My friend and I jumped back in the trucks to monitor the light from flames over the not-too-distant hill. We drove toward the freeway and saw that the fire and flames were still far enough in the distance for us to remain at home a little longer. I realized I was almost out of gas, so we went to the gas station, and while I was at the pump covering my mouth from the unbreathable air, I heard a loud voice from a police car racing through the streets, saying, "Evacuate evacuate, it's mandatory!" This was a moment in time that seemed apocalyptic. My worst nightmare realized: the fire had jumped the freeway.

WHAT? My friend and I raced back to the house and to our husbands who were frantically and methodically loading the horses into the trainers. I rapidly started packing the rest of my things and woke my children, instructing them to grab their emergency provisions so that we could evacuate—fast.

I was still calm as I knew the fire was relatively far away. Just then, my husband raced through the door of my bedroom. Out of breath, he looked at me, his face filled with fear, and said, "I can see the fire! It's on the hill. It's here, in front of our house." He yelled, "I'm loading the horses, we have to go now, now!" I ran outside, saw flames, and gasped for air as I said to my kids, "Hurry! Run! We have to go now, now!" Just then a friend called, and I will never forget those terrible words as I picked up the phone: "My house is burning!" She was inconsolably terrified. "I'm being evacuated. I can see the fire. It's here." I shouted to everyone, "We have to go, now, we are out of time." The kids were now frantic as we piled dogs, turtles, bunnies, and a chameleon into the cars. My middle daughter was hosing off the pool deck in her earnest attempts to stave off the flames. I told her to go into the house as she could hardly breathe. The air was impenetrably laden with lung-damaging ash. I grabbed the hose and began to spray our pool deck, and pray that God would spare our home, that as He commands the winds and IS the creator of the universe, that HIS sovereign hand would spare our land and home that we had dedicated to him. My sister kept calling me and said that God had repeatedly reminded her: "Get everything wet. I keep hearing get everything wet." So I did.

I raced back into the home, grabbed my suitcase, and we drove both cars down to the barn and then proceeded to load all of our own chickens and our friends' chickens, goats, and horses, then headed back up the hill and out to safety. Just then I realized that the word "safety" might be a fantasy. Where would we be safe? All the freeways were closed north and south. The road to the right closed, and the only road still open was straight towards the beach. Upon leaving, my heart sank as we left some of the horses in our back pasture with all of the neighbors' horses who were awaiting trailers to come back to get them. Once again I prayed fervently, almost yelling: "Father, please protect and cover our animals and home with the blood of Jesus."

As we were leaving there were approximately twenty fire trucks headed down our street. It was our first sign of hope that we so desperately needed. We headed out down the only road we could access—the road that would lead us to the Pacific Ocean. While driving down the highway, we could see flames in the distance on the large mountain-scape. I asked my girls to join me aloud and pray for the people, mountains, hills, our land, our home, and animals. We called our friends, the Myers, and asked them if we could come to their home for safety, as they lived by the beach, until the fires were out and we could go home. They welcomed us with our horses, dogs, chickens, and all the other animals with open arms.

No sooner had we eaten breakfast and started to relax when the phones began to scream again. I was shocked. What now? The fires had begun to make their way to the beach in Malibu and now our friends were being evacuated. This didn't seem real as the sun had just come up and it was only 7:00 am. As they began to gather their belongings, we decided to take the horses and animals to the beach to the "safe zone" that was designated by the city. We hugged our friends goodbye. While traveling to the ocean the sky became darker and darker with smoke, we finally got to the beach with all forty-five animals. Our kids were happy as they were finally able to ride their horses on the beach which had been a fantasy of theirs, but it was such an ominous feeling—watching the smoke get closer and closer, blacker and blacker. In fact, a news crew that was on the beach asked if they could do a quick story on us and the kids on their horses now riding on the beach. After about an hour or so went by, more people started arriving. All kinds of animals were now on the beach: horses, goats, turtles, dogs. People brought llamas, donkeys, cats, and camels. It was a surreal scene, like nothing I have ever experienced before.

Suddenly, we looked up and could see the flames begin to burn a home on the other side of Pacific Coast Highway not too far away from us. My husband and I looked at each other and said, "Let's go!" It was no longer safe there. We loaded everyone and every animal once again into the cars and went down the crowded two-lane Pacific Coast Highway. At times, the flames were on the left side of us, and we felt like sitting ducks. I called ahead to a barn we had once boarded our horses, and they graciously gave us stalls for three of the horses we were able to take with us. It took us six hours to make an hour-and-a-half drive.

Once we were out of the fire zone, we stopped at a gas station to fill up our tank and replenish our water stocks. Full of gratitude and relief, tears began to stream down my face. I felt as though we had been through a mini-war and that we were finally safe. The fire was nowhere in sight and there was such a sense of relief. We finally got the horses to safety, settled them in the barn, and headed to friends who had kindly already set up spaces for us and the rest of our animals.

When we arrived at our friends', our relief was partial this time as we watched the news and saw the fire encircling our town and the mountains nearby and around our home. I prayed that God would spare and protect all of the horses that were still in the huge arena near our creek, as well as our neighbors and all the homes. I called so many people with trailers to try to get the last of our horses evacuated, but none of them could get in to get the horses out to safety as the fire was now upon them and the streets were all shut down. Once again my heart sank, but I still trusted and believed God for a miracle.

The next day my husband announced he was going back to the house as soon as the sun arose. Knowing the streets and freeways were still blocked by police, I asked him how he planned to do that. He said he didn't know but he had had enough, so he left. I took the girls to see their horses at the other stable, which was a good distraction from all the devastation and chaos. At this point, we still did not know if our home was going to be there or not, or what happened to the horses, all the phones and all the internet was out. Finally, we got the call and the picture from a friend who rode his bike through the police barricade and showed us that the horses and our entire property was safe. Not a leaf from a tree was out of place. It was an absolute miracle.

My kids and I decided to head back to the house late that evening as we heard they were letting residents back in. My husband made it in, and in a brief moment of cellular service, he was able to show us photographs of the devastation all around. He and I cried together over the phone, so thankful that God had spared our home, our neighbor's homes, and our property.

The destruction in our area was heartbreaking. By the time we made it to our street that evening, the police were now out in full force and had blocked off all access into our area as power lines were down and there were still small spot fires happening. Determined to get home, I told my husband that we were stuck behind police cars, the road was completely blocked, and there was no way to get home now. He advised me to park the car at a designated spot, and he would come to fetch us. His added advice was that when we grabbed all the animals that were with us, we should run as fast as possible to his waiting car before anyone could stop us! That's exactly what we did, and the police were gracious and turned the other way when they saw our family running with armloads of animals to his car, so our family could reunite. It was another miracle from God.

We were so grateful to be home, have a home, and be together. My daughter, who is older and lives out of state, was beside herself as she watched helplessly from afar.

As the sun came up on a new day, I got out of bed and took a deep breath to see the toll the fire took on the land surrounding us. I opened the window, and as I looked upon the devastation, I fell to my knees and began to sob in thanksgiving that our property was spared, but also in horror at the loss I was witnessing of the land and the homes and lives that were gone. I went to the kids, instructed them to put on breathing masks, and we walked out the front door. Across the street, all we saw was the charred blackness from the fire. It was merciless, but God had been infinitely merciful with our home. The fire literally stopped at the street by our front door and stopped at our back fence where all those precious horses were. It was truly a miracle. The vinyl fences which should have melted away were still white and intact, and the crosses on the property were still unmoved; even though the fire came right to the base of the wood cross, no fire touched it. All of the horses were saved. Upon looking at the line where the fire stopped, I felt as though it was literally as if Jesus Christ himself was standing there saying, "STOP. Go no further." My sister had said she was praying this verse over us and our property.

> They saw that the fire had not harmed their bodies, nor was the hair of their heads singed; their robes were not scorched, and there was no smell of fire on them. (Daniel 3:27 NIV)

I'm so glad God called me to "pre-pray" before the fire even hit. When we first bought this home and property, I would walk up the hills surrounding our home and pray, cry out to God, face the hills, and speak to them in prayer. Honestly, I felt like a crazy woman half of the time. I didn't understand why I felt this burning in my spirit to pray over and around our property. I would take my Bible and encircle our area. I would read my "Book of Promises" in every area and every corner of our land and beyond. Now I know God was asking me to "pre-pray" before disaster struck. I would decree and declare safety around the borders of our home and speak life against what the enemy wanted to kill. I always tell the girls in the Bible study I teach: read God's word, speak God's word, get in agreement with God's word, believe God's word, and then watch God work. I believe with all my heart those prayers helped save our home and all of the animals, but I must make this clear that even if God had not rescued our home, God is still God, and He would have worked something good out of it! I'm so thankful I didn't try to reason in my mind why I was so burdened to pray so many of those days and that I simply prayed out of obedience.

They say you can tell a lot about a person by what they value. Upon unpacking, I realized I learned some things about myself as well. I didn't grab my expensive clothes or purses. Instead, I took my Bible, my cowboy boots, important papers, and some pictures of my children and family. Witnessing the unwieldy forces of nature was a very large wake-up call for me to prioritize the important things in life. If we are quiet enough to listen to God, He will faithfully walk us through frightening episodes life throws at us and make us stronger, wiser people who are overcomers.

Prayer

Dear Lord, we know evil exists. We know you have the power over the wind and the waves, that you are sovereign over all the earth. You are greater than anyone or anything in this world. We refuse to bow to fear and hate against our brothers and sisters. We can only truly love through the endless power of the love of Jesus Christ. We will begin to forgive freely, as you become greater in us and we become less. Let the love of God ignite a firestorm of love and forgiveness with all whom we come in contact. Red, yellow, black, and white; we are all precious in your sight.

Challenge Questions

1. What would you take if you had only a short time to evacuate your home?

2. When you are surrounded by fire, you can either pray or panic, live in faith or fear. What scripture would you choose when you are in a similar state of crisis?

3. What is the most important thing in your life and why? Are there perhaps other things that seem important that you could leave behind?

4. Ask yourself this question: does my lifestyle, my prayer life, and my buying or giving, help or hurt others around me? What is one thing I can do this week to help someone who may be helpless?

5. Read Psalm 91 aloud. Declare it over yourself and loved ones.

Trust

20

The Great Awakening

JUST LIKE A TREE is planted for a purpose, so are prayers. They are sent out into the atmosphere for a great and mighty purpose. When we plant a tree, we are generally planting the tree for shade, beauty, to purify the air, or to bear fruit, so in the same way, it is with our prayers that we pray.

I really identify with nature in such a profound way. I believe God speaks to us through nature. If we would only take the time to stop, look, and listen, He will reveal deep, undiscovered secrets through nature. For example, did you know a healthy tree sucks all the harmful greenhouse gases from the air and, in turn, releases life-giving carbon dioxide back into the toxic air making it purer? It works just the same way as we release our prayers from our mouths. Those prayers pour life into the toxic atmosphere, suck all of the harmful toxins from your life, cause the enemy to flee, and then release an atmosphere of peace and healing. Just as a tree holds the soil in place, our prayers also ground us and hold our relationship with God in place. Prayer is our 911 hotline directly to God, twenty-four hours a day, seven days a week.

I'm not generally a person who likes labels. Recently, through the destructive nature of this pandemic that has fallen across our entire world, in certain parts of the United States, governors and mayors have themselves determined what and who is considered essential and non-essential. Imagine that, all of a sudden churches and businesses are closed with no reopening in sight, as churches, pastors, and worship leaders are considered non-essential. Singing in a church here in California was declared by the governor as dangerous, non-essential, or a super spreader, all the while people have flooded our streets standing practically on top of one another in protests, much of the time with no face protection. Businesses remain closed and lives have been destroyed from the plague and financial ruin. I understand being safe and considerate of others, but with our churches and many businesses closed indefinitely, let's make a decision right now to be "super spreaders" of God's word, love, life, grace, and mercy. Let us *Rise Up!*, take a tragic moment in this time in our world, and turn it into triumph and victory through the power of God.

> It just takes one to throw a stone upon a sleepy lake to ripple on.
> (Brenda Epperson-Moore and Steve Bertrand, "One")

When the plague and pandemic hit, I felt as though I had to do something. I knew this was a "forced pause" for humanity; COVID is the great equalizer. The single unifying remnant of the pandemic is that we are all going through the same thing at once. Worldwide, more people are praying than were ever before recorded. This is a time for each of us to examine our lives to become the best version of ourselves and improve the world around us. As graffiti messages of hate were sprayed on our local city walls and buildings and my anger and frustration began to build, I realized I needed to repent, pray and fast; otherwise, I would be no better than the same angry people spreading hate and causing chaos. Remember to be very, very wary of any movement that causes hate, division, fear, and lawlessness. Any of those byproducts of a movement should make us all pause and step on the brakes before we mindlessly follow. The race relations movement has been crying out for justice and reform. The abuse and imbalance of power should be exposed and seems to be coming to a head. While there are wonderful peaceful protests, there are also thugs and much lawlessness that is stealing, killing, destroying neighborhoods, and taking over our streets. I am passionate about my life and your life being a solution.

When we exchange the truth for a lie, we become blinded. Therefore, we must secure the truth of God's word in our heart as absolute truth, because when we do not differentiate good from evil, destruction and devastation will surely follow.

> Woe to those who call evil good and good evil. (Isaiah 5:20 NIV)

I believe there is a world changer in all of us. A world changer is committed to standing up and speaking up for others. During quarantine, this book and our podcast, "Morning Cup of Faith," were both born. Ascend Women, which I am the Founding Co-Director of, was one of the last events to take place in the state of California before the world shut down.

The power of God fell upon the women that day in March 2020. While the world was closing up, we remained open. The spirit of God was released, and His presence and anointing on the women allowed deep inner healing to take place in many of their lives. God does not conform to the limitations of the world. He is endless. He is not confined by space or time. At our event that day, women's lives were healed and empowered to move on and move forward. As they walked out the door of this new unknown pandemic season, they left enabled and filled with His might and strength. I'll never forget how the women one by one walked in that day. We were not sure if anyone would actually even show up because the pandemic hit so hard. There were lines at the grocery store and gas station; people began to panic and fill carts with food, and of course, toilet paper, fearing we would not have enough food to eat. Some of the women walked in with a smile on their faces, full of *joy* and confidence, while others walked in full of fear and trepidation. God met us all that day. Come just as you are, whether you barely have enough strength and are crawling to the foot of the cross or you are full of assurance. God will meet you and heal you right where you are.

> You are only one decision away from a totally different life.
> (Zig Ziglar)

The world might tell you who you are and what you do is not enough or "non-essential," but in God's kingdom you are *absolutely* essential, and through Him, you will always have enough. There are no non-essential people in God's kingdom; there is no social distancing with God. All through the Bible, God uses the broken, the bruised, the forgotten, the lost, and the fallen, but God rarely uses the failures, because failures have given up. They refuse to believe and cease to step ahead. If you or someone you know has given up, then believe for them. Be the reassurance they need. We must never ever give in to the lie that anyone or anything is hopeless. We must never give up on God. Remember, He never gives up on us.

> You never fail until you stop trying. (Albert Einstein)

One secret about me is I've always been addicted to power. I am so attracted to powerful people, powerful cars, the most powerful animals, airplanes; anything that represents power draws me into it. So then I ask you: if you are like me, why not plug into the ultimate power, Jesus Christ, the One who fills us with *joy*, the One who created everything, the heavens, and earth, and then rested on the seventh day. That's power! I am challenging you to plug into the omnipotent, sovereign strength of God, who has the authority and power over the surging waves and the infinite solar system. Is there anything more powerful than God? No!

> Love sees no color, love has no form, love wraps its arms around
> the world until it's reborn.
> (Brenda Epperson-Moore and Tim Miner, "Reborn")

Poverty has increased exponentially, as the financial crisis and consequences of this pandemic has ripped lives apart and poured vast uncertainty into our economy. Sadly, the death toll is rising along with financial poverty and despair. There is also rampant spiritual poverty that is evident. We cannot as a society turn a blind eye and continue to accommodate wickedness; this plague is a wake-up call for all humanity. We have forgotten God; therefore, we have forgotten who we are. We are spiritually numb and dumb, and we have filled our minds, ears, and heart with everything BUT God. Throughout the Bible, anytime a nation took God from their land and hearts and built idols, worshipped false gods, and did detestable things in the sight of the Lord, devastation was sure to follow.

> Now I am about to go the way of all the earth. You know with all
> your heart and soul that not one of all the good promises the Lord
> God gave you has failed. Every promise has been fulfilled; not one
> has failed. But just as all the good things the Lord your God has
> promised you have come to you, so he will bring on you all the evil
> things he has threatened, until the Lord your God has destroyed
> you from this good land he has given you. If you violate the cov-
> enant of the Lord your God, which he commanded you, and go
> and serve other gods and bow down to them, the Lord's anger will
> burn against you, and you will quickly perish from the good land
> he has given you. (Joshua 23:14–16 NIV)

Do not fret. Do not fear. There is always hope. As a hinge on a door is essential, your gifts and talents are essential right now for such a time as this. The hinge on a door allows a door to be able to open and pivot. Without the hinges, a door simply won't open. An open door from God is a gateway for God to do His mighty works in and through our lives. I have this burning in my heart and soul to be a handle on the door that opens and unleashes the floodgates of endless possibilities into your soul.

Do you know the difference between a thermostat and a thermometer? A thermometer *tells you* the temperature in the room while a thermostat regulates the temperature in a room. I want you and I to be so filled with the Holy Spirit that when we walk in a room, like a thermostat, we change the environment. I want my life and yours to cause the dark to become light. As we decree and declare His goodness from our mouth, His life is breathed into our souls. Let's live our life like a thermostat which is considered *smart* because a thermostat constantly has a read on what's happening in its environment; when the room is too cold, emotionless, and lifeless, it adds a warm breeze of encouragement, love, and *joy*. If the room is too hot with frustration and anger, the thermostat adds just enough cool air to revitalize people and cool them off which allows them to regain insight, compassion, and vision once again. Let's become the thermostats of change in our home, family, school, workplace, and world.

> See, I set before you today life and prosperity, death and destruction. For I command you today to love the Lord your God, to walk in obedience to him, and to keep his commands, decrees and laws; then you will live and increase, and the Lord your God will bless you in the land you are entering to possess.
> (Deuteronomy 30:15–20 NIV)

As I mentioned earlier, by nature I've always been a bit rebellious. I tend to ask a ton of questions and not immediately trust just anyone. Remember I'm a work in progress just like you. I sometimes tend to be a bit skeptical and not one to immediately just follow along with what others are doing and saying. If you're like me, then dive deep into prayer and into God's arms. Make your relationship with Him yours alone. Don't just believe me, try Him, and see for yourself what He will uncover in your life that will allow you the fullness of *joy*. So if you're a bit of a rebel and going to rebel against something, rebel against what the world says is right when it doesn't line up with the word of God, rebel against what pop culture says is "right or acceptable," when you know it's causing pain in others, and rebel against pride, vanity, godlessness, and self-sufficiency. Don't just mindlessly follow others. Why are you trying to "fit in," when God has created you to stand out?

You may say, "I just don't hear God." Oftentimes, we do not hear because we defile ourselves with detestable things. We place other people or idols or materialism in front of God. We bow to the altar of social media. We bow to the altar of beauty. We bow to the god of mammon (money). We make excuses for our actions. We blur the line between right and wrong, good and evil, because, without God, our moral compass is broken and pointed in the wrong direction.

God wants us to *Rise Up* and become leaders, not mindless followers. We must stop, pray, wait, believe, and cut our teeth on the idea that pop culture may not be our answer. God is our answer. Take a moment to possibly consider that pop culture may be one of the very things increasing your anxiety and robbing you of your happiness. Don't just accept the complacency of what the world says is right or wrong. The Bible calls us to be in the world, not of the world.

While we don't know how or when this pandemic will all end, we do know the one who knows the beginning from the end. "Look to the Lord and His strength and seek His face always" (Psalm 105:4 NIV). God always surprises us, he may not come when we want him to, but He's always right on time. As darkness and hate try to divide let's all *Rise Up* together in love and unity, so evil and division will not prevail.

I am constantly anointing everything with oil, my house, children, animals everything, do the same anoint your surroundings, and allow the love of God to give peace to the unrest.

Get excited and welcome the great awakening happening in the world today. I am hopeful that revival will break out; even though churches are closed, we will bring the church to the streets to meet the people where they are. Let the heavens reign down signs and wonders to release revival, eradicate darkness, and slay Satan, so all can live free. Not only do we need to clean our hands during this pandemic, we also need to clean and purify our hearts, so we can see clearly and hear what God is saying. I believe God has set something wonderful in motion for you. Allow Him to uncover the dark spots in your life so you can move into the light. Stay rooted in Jesus during this time of uncertainty. Stay in the calm, and remain in the eye of the storm with your eyes on Jesus so you will not be tossed in the troubled culture, wind and sea.

> God is our refuge and strength, always ready to help in times of trouble. (Ephesians 46:1 NIV)

Be blessed in the mess because God does his most effective work in the last moments when we least expect it. Remain in *joy*, remain in faith, remain assured, and confident that God *will* work good in this time. In today's tumultuous culture, sometimes we have to fight to find our *joy* but do it anyway.

I have learned that I am capable of more than what I can see right in front of me. I have learned that there is a sea of people who need our help. I have learned that we cannot have the fullness of life and purpose and peace if we leave God out of our life. So, whatever is in your hands in your mind or heart to do or give, no matter how big or small, be assured it will be a blessing to a world that has forgotten to pray, so it has fallen *prey* to the enemy. No matter what you have been through, even if you have been through hell, remember you have heaven on the inside of you, which is endless unstoppable power and resource that will release and unlock all you need to *Rise Up* and out of your seat of complacency. Never give up on serving others and engaging in humanity just like Jesus did. This will overflow your cup with *joy* unspeakable and full of that powerful "*joy* wave" glory that will overtake and overcome any circumstance you may be facing. Remember, it's okay to glance at your problem, but keep your gaze upon God.

> The name of the Lord is a strong tower; the righteous run into it and are safe. (Psalm 18:10 NIV)

Prayer

Dear God in heaven, we beseech your love to fall on our land and into our hearts. Let us be imperfectly beautiful together. Thank you for accepting me into your family. I will be quick to forgive and slow to anger. Help me to *Rise Up* and walk away from division, anger, and hate toward my fellow man, and step into the fullness of peace and *joy* you have for my life. I will not fear the darkness. I will be the thermostat of change. I speak life, blessings, prosperity and radical transformation over your life. Heal our hearts, heal our land, and heal our mind. Ignite the fire of the Holy Spirit in our soul and radically transform us and the world, as the birthing pains of revival burst forth into every tongue, every tribe, and every nation. Amen.

Congratulations you have graduated! I'm so proud of you. Answer these last few questions and allow the Holy Spirit to soak your heart and mind. Thank you for participating with me on this brand-new journey. God has seen your heart and the work you have put into finding a life full of *joy*. Thank you for believing in me and allowing me the opportunity to encourage you and pour life into your tender heart. What an honor it has been. Please reach out to me and let me know what God has done for you and how I can further encourage you! Even though I don't know you, I really do love you!

Challenge Questions

1. What is something you need to take a risk on? Write it down, be daring, and go for it.

2. Spiritual cleansing must reach deep into our hearts, it is a job only God can do if we allow Him full access into our lives. Is there an area in your life you are holding back from God that he needs full access to? Submit, trust, and allow God to remove the stain of sin from your life.

3. Write down three "*joy* strategies" you can implement in your life today, and do them. Here are some ideas: Take a long walk on a beautiful path; Recall a happy time or occasion; Write three things you love about yourself.

4. What is a practical step you can take today to "sanitize" your hands and heart? Maybe stop listening to hours of news? Start listening to praise music.

5. How can you anoint your lips with grace rather than hate?

6. Who can you call or text today that needs to hear your voice?

7. What is God showing you to turn *from* so you can easily turn *to* Him? Or are you more worried about what others think rather than what God thinks?

8. How can you empower those around you to increase their faith? To uplift their heart's? Maybe a complete stranger needs a kind word? Do it afraid if you have to.

Author's Platform

Today, Brenda Epperson-Moore's life is a testament to her faith. She attained worldwide recognition through the eight years she played Ashley Abbott on CBS's daytime drama, *The Young and the Restless*. She signed with Sony/Tristar Music label and became the opening act for Lionel Richie's world tour. Her many trips to the Cannes Film Festivals involved promoting the movies that she starred in. She rubbed shoulders with Hollywood A-list people while working on her extensive movie career. *Rise Up!* is her first book in the IJOY series.

In sharing parts of her life, Brenda is encouraging everyone who has ever experienced loss, rejection, loneliness, hopelessness, doubt, insecurity and injustice to realize that nothing is impossible through God. Even when immense challenges tempt us to quit, the harvest at the end of the tunnel is usually far greater than we can envisage.

Brenda took her bible as a young girl and realized that, through the days in which she felt death-like, there was an infinite power that would relinquish her of her sorrows, fears, and tears. The promise of God's power was real.

About the Author

BRENDA EPPERSON-MOORE IS AN actress, singer, host, and writer who achieved early fame as Ashley Abbott, the lead character in CBS's *The Young the Restless*. Born in North Hollywood, California, she is the daughter of famed musician and actor, Don Epperson, who suffered an untimely death when Brenda was six years old. She is a Sony/TriStar recording artist and was the opening act for Lionel Richie during his World *Time* tour. Brenda won the "Angel Award" for the song "If You Believe," a duet she recorded with Phillip Ingram. She was a television host and co-hosted a beauty show with Dr. Andrew Ordon from the television show *The Doctors*. She has also appeared on many popular shows including *Howie Mandel* and *Oprah*. With an extensive movie career Brenda has traveled the world working with A-list actors. Brenda has graced the covers of *Woman's World Magazine, Soap Opera Digest,* and *TV Guide,* and she has had extensive stories in *People Magazine, USA Today,* and countless other publications. In 2012, God tapped Brenda on the shoulder and told her to start a non-profit women's conference, she is the founding Co-Director of an uplifting, faith-based movement for women: *AscendWomen.org.* Brenda takes her passion, talents, and her entertainment industry connections to outreach programs and organizations that touch the lives of the broken, battered, and abused. She is the contributing author to the book *Blessedness of Brokenness* (2012). Brenda is currently in her fourth year on UMC Urban Channel, *The Rich and the Ruthless,* playing the character Edith Norman. Brenda is a sought after speaker and sings nationwide using her international platform to encourage, empower, and remind us all that *joy* and the indomitable power of God is attainable for all of us. She is married to the love of her life and is raising three beautiful daughters.

You can reach out to Brenda:

www.BrendaEpperson.com
Instagram @BrendaEpperson2
Facebook Page @JustBrendaEpperson
Twitter @BrendaEpperson
Her Music can be downloaded on iTunes and Soundcloud
www.AscendWomen.org
Facebook @AscendWomen
Instagram @AscendWomen
Instagram @MorningCupofFaith
Podcast: Morning Cup of Faith

Bibliography

Baylor College of Medicine. "Baby's Smile Is A Natural High." *ScienceDaily*, July 8, 2008. www.sciencedaily.com/releases/2008/07/080707081852.htm.

Bible Study Tools. "Fowler." https://www.biblestudytools.com/encyclopedias/isbe/fowler.html.

Colbert, Don. *Deadly Emotions: Understand the Mind-Body-Spirit Connection that Can Heal or Destroy You.* Nashville: Nelson, 2020.

Elias, Marilyn. "Hugs Warm the Heart, and May Protect It." *USA Today*, March 10, 2003. http://usatoday30.usatoday.com/news/health/2003-3-09-hug-usat_x.htm.

Furnas, Wendell Jess. "Obituaries." *Santa Paula Times*, December 9, 2011. https://santapaulatimes.com/news/archivestory.php/aid/24334/Obituaries.html.

Gardner, Sarah, and Dave Albee. "Study Focuses on Strategies for Achieving Goals, Resolutions." Press release no. 266, February 1, 2015. https://scholar.dominican.edu/news-releases/266.

Gordon, Devin. "John Wooden: First, How To Put On Your Socks." *Newsweek*, October 24, 1999. https://www.newsweek.com/john-wooden-first-how-put-your-socks-167942.

Hinman, Al. "Study: Well-hugged Babies Make Less-stressed Adults." *CNN*, September 11, 1997. http://www.cnn.com/HEALTH/9709/11/nfm.touch.stress/.

Holmes, Lindsay. "7 Reasons Why We Should Be Giving More Hugs." *Huffington Post*, December 6, 2017. https://www.huffpost.com/entry/health-benefits-of-huggin_n_5008616.

Koole, Sander L. "Touch May Alleviate Existential Fears for People With Low Self-Esteem." *Association for Physical Science*, November 6, 2013. https://www.psychologicalscience.org/news/releases/touch-may-alleviate-existential-fears-for-people-with-low-self-esteem.html.

Leaf, Caroline. *Who Switched Off My Brain? Controlling Toxic Thoughts and Emotions.* Nashville: Nelson, 2009.

Lemonick, Michael D. "Health: The Biology of Joy." *Time*, January 9, 2005. http://content.time.com/time/magazine/article/0,9171,1015863,00.html.

Mineo, Liz. "Good Genes Are Nice, but Joy Is Better." *Harvard Gazette*, April 11, 2017. https://news.harvard.edu/gazette/story/2017/04/over-nearly-80-years-harvard-study-has-been-showing-how-to-live-a-healthy-and-happy-life/.

Osteen, Joel. "Become a Miracle." http://www.sermonly.com/14/joel-osteen-become-a-miracle/7014/.

Osteen-Comes, Lisa. *You Are Made for More!: How to Become All You Were Created to Be.* New York: FaithWords, 2012.

Bibliography

Ramachandran, V. S. *A Brief Tour of Human Consciousness: From Imposter Poodles to Purple Numbers*. London: Pi, 2004.

Santi, Jenny. "The Secret to Happiness Is Helping Others." *TIME*. https://time.com/collection/guide-to-happiness/4070299/secret-to-happiness/.

Sternbergh, Adam. "How to Be Happy." *The Cut*. https://www.thecut.com/2018/05/how-to-be-happy.html.

CPSIA information can be obtained
at www.ICGtesting.com
Printed in the USA
FSHW022257190421
80637FS